Life and Work at Sea

BY THE SAME AUTHOR

The Battle for Reform, 1815–1832, Lutterworth, 1973

A Day in the Life of a Victorian Factory Worker, Allen and Unwin, 1973

A Day in the Life of a Victorian Farm Worker, Allen and Unwin, 1972

Farming, A. & C. Black, 2nd ed., 1970

Factory Life and Work, Harrap, 1973 (uniform with this volume)

How it Happened, Blackwell, 1971

Travel and Communications, Harrap, 1972

What they've said about . . . Nineteenth-century Reformers, Oxford University Press, 1971

What they've said about . . . Nineteenth-century Statesmen, Oxford University Press, 1972

A Short History of Farming, Macmillan, 1970

The Past, Present and Future of
Life and Work at Sea

A DOCUMENTARY INQUIRY

by Frank E. Huggett

HARRAP   LONDON

First published in Great Britain 1975
by George G. Harrap & Co. Ltd
182–184 High Holborn, London WC1V 7AX

©*Frank E. Huggett* 1975

ISBN 0 245 51943 2

*Composed in Baskerville type and printed
by J. W. Arrowsmith Ltd, Bristol
Made in Great Britain*

Preface

Britain has long depended on the Royal Navy as its first line of defence, and on its merchant navy for the growth of trade and the import of raw materials and the export of manufactured goods, without which it could not have become a great industrial power. Until the last century there was no distinction between the men who manned the warships and those seamen in the merchant vessels. Seamen were pressed into service in the Royal Navy in times of need. This book describes the life and work of sailors from the first voyages of discovery and adventure and the defeat of the Spanish Armada, to modern times—often in the words of the men from the lower deck themselves.

There are eight parts, each of which is divided into four sections as follows:

(1) gives contemporary accounts from many different sources, with a linking commentary, of the main development in life and work at sea during the period;

(2) also gives a large number of extracts from contemporary accounts, dealing mainly with improvements made in conditions;

(3) assesses the importance of the changes;

(4) gives a list of the more important dates, and books for further reading.

There is also a fuller bibliography at the end of the book, a glossary of some common maritime terms, and details of some museums and societies.

Contents

List of Illustrations

Part One

Adventurers and Discoverers

1

The sailor has always had a hard and dangerous but adventurous life. In the past a boy or a young man might go to sea for many different reasons: to escape from the law, a broken love-affair or the monotonous routine of daily life; to see the world or to seek his fortune; or simply because he was born in a port and his father and his grandfather had 'used the sea' before him. What kept him at sea was sometimes the fact that he knew no other way of life, but more often because he had an inexhaustible fund of curiosity and optimism. He wanted to see one more foreign country, to give himself one more chance to make his fortune, before he gave up the sea. By that time he was a real sailor.

A nobleman who made a voyage as a passenger through the Mediterranean in the sixteenth century came back full of admiration for sailors.

> What state of life, friendly reader, can be harder, think you, than that of mariners? How many heats and colds must they endure? How often must they be frighted with thunder and lightning, and daily, nay, hourly, exposed to the violence of the winds and rains? How often must they be tormented with hunger and thirst, and poisoned up with dirt and nastiness, their lodging being no better than a prison, having little or no furniture, and if any, very nasty, hard bedding, coarse diet, and such as require iron teeth to devour it, stinking drink, dirty clothes, inconvenience of all sorts, restless nights, and ever unquiet in the open air? Not to mention their perpetual banishment from their native homes, being exiles, wanderers, stragglers, in perpetual motion; deprived of all the enjoyment and society of a wife and children. . . .
>
> *(The Travels of Martin Baumgarten, A Nobleman of Germany, through Egypt, Arabia, Palestine and Syria,* London, 1594)

The 'coarse diet' and the 'stinking drink' were to be two of the main grievances of sailors right up to the present century. In theory, sailors in Royal warships had adequate rations by the standards of those times:

> Every man and boy is allowed a pound of bread a day.
> Every man and boy is allowed a gallon of beer a day, that is to say, a quart in the morning, a quart at dinner, a quart in the afternoon, and a quart at supper.
> Every man and boy is allowed a day, on flesh days, one pound of beef, or else one pound of pork with pease, that is, on Sunday, Monday, Tuesday and Thursday. On fish days, every mess, which is four men, are allowed a side of salt fish, either haberdine,[1] ling, or cod, seven ounces of butter, and fourteen ounces of cheese, Friday excepted, on which day they have but half allowance.
>
> (Sir William Monson: *Naval Tracts*, London, 1732)

But the sailors frequently did not receive their full rations. Sometimes, the private contractor who supplied the food conspired with the ship's officers—the purser, the cook or the captain—to cheat the men by providing smaller amounts and splitting the profit between them. On longer voyages, when food became short, six sailors commonly had to subsist on four men's rations. On the longest voyages of discovery, the men sometimes went ashore to catch rats, monkeys, birds, and even penguins.

The quality of the food was usually atrocious. Horse-meat was often substituted for beef, and a few nails and horse's hooves were thrown in for good measure. When Richard Chancellor set out on a voyage of discovery in 1553 he

> was not a little grieved with the feare of wanting victuals, part whereof was found to be corrupt and putrified at Harwiche, and the hoggesheads of wine also leaked. . . .
>
> (Clement Adams: 'The Newe Navigation and Discoverie of the Kingdome of Moscovia, by the Northeast in the yeere 1553', in Richard Hakluyt: *The Principal Navigations, Voyages and Discoveries of the English Nation*, London, 1589)

The quality of the other rations was just as bad. The beer was often flat and sour; the cheese, wrapped in muslin, was either so hard that sailors carved it into model ships, or it was soft and crawling with maggots; the butter, stored in wooden casks, was rancid; and the

---

[1] Salted cod.

bread was the traditional 'hard tack'—ship's biscuits which were as hard as iron.

The sailors lived in perpetual discomfort in these small, creaking, top-heavy Tudor ships, which rolled and pitched in even the slightest sea. They were on duty seven days a week, working alternately in watches. But whenever there was a sudden storm or some other danger—which was frequent enough—all hands were called upon to help, whether they were off duty or not. While they were working the men got wet through to the skin. They worked in bare feet, and often had only one suit of clothes, which was soon torn into tattered rags. A few private ships provided a livery, or uniform, to be worn on special occasions.

> Item, The liveries in apparel given to the mariners be to be kept by the Marchants, and not to be worne, but by the order of the Captaine, when hee shall see cause to muster or shewe them in good array, for the advancement and honour of the voyage. . . .
>
> ('The excellent orders and instructions of Sebastian Cabot given to Sir Hugh Willoughby and his Fleete in their voyage intended for Cathay', in Richard Hakluyt, op. cit.)

And early in the sixteenth century some Royal warships started to carry stocks of clothes—canvas tunics and breeches lined with cotton; shirts; woollen and worsted stockings; woollen caps. But the sailor had to buy them out of his wages.

In their rare intervals of rest the men had nowhere to sleep but the bare deck. Most captains banned the use of straw mattresses because they increased the fire risk on these wooden ships; hammocks, which were copied from the string nets used by some inhabitants of the West Indies, were not introduced until the end of the sixteenth century.

These overcrowded ships were floating slums in which disease of all kinds spread rapidly. The men rarely washed. Fleas, which carry plague, and lice, which carry typhus, abounded. There was an overpowering smell from the bilges, where the filth of many years accumulated. The only sanitary facilities were the 'heads'—an open part of the deck in the bow. The lack of fresh fruit and vegetables in their diet caused thousands of sailors to die of scurvy on the longer voyages.

> It bringeth with it a great desire to drinke, and causeth a general swelling of all parts of the body, especially of the legges and gummes, and many time the teeth fall out of the jawes without paine. The signes to

know this disease in the beginning are divers, by the swelling of the gummes, by denting the flesh of the legges with a mans finger, the pit remaining without filling up in a good space; others show it with their lasinesses, others complaine of the cricke of the backe etc. all which, are for the most part, certaine tokens of infection. . . . In twentie yeeres (since I have used the Sea) I dare take upon me, to give account of ten thousand men consumed with this disease.

(*The Observations of Sir Richard Hawkins, Knight, in his Voyage into the South Sea*, London, 1593)

It is little wonder that on longer voyages it was quite common for half the crew or more to die of disease, which was a bigger killer than any enemy's guns right up to the nineteenth century.

In Tudor times there was far less distinction between ships—and their crews—than there is today. The sea was an open battlefield in times of war, and even in times of peace merchant ships had to be able to protect themselves against the pirates who haunted the coasts and creeks of England. For this reason, even the smallest merchant vessels, of 50 tons or so, which were used mainly in the coastal trade and in voyages to neighbouring countries like France and Holland, carried a few guns. Some of the larger merchant ships were almost as well armed as warships, carrying muzzle-loading culverins, long-range 18-pounders and iron or brass demi-cannon, which could hurl a 30 lb shot a mile or more.

The worst conditions for sailors were to be found in Royal ships, which were owned or commissioned by the monarch. Wages were much lower than in merchant vessels, and were often many months, or even years, in arrears. At the end of the sixteenth century the merchant seaman was being paid 17s. to 18s. a month, but his counterpart in the Royal ships was getting only 10s. When a warship captured an enemy vessel the sailors had a chance to make a little extra money.

I find that in Queen Elizabeth's time, in the taking of any prize, all that was found upon the upper orlop[2] was allowed to be the mariners' and soldiers'. . . .

(W. G. Perrin, editor: *Boteler's Dialogues* (1685), Navy Records Society, 1929)

But this pillage was rarely worth much, even when sailors disobeyed orders by landing on the enemy's soil and going inland

three or four miles, in hope only to pillage some rotten household stuff. And I did see one of these make his brave retreat with a feather bed on his

[2] Deck.

back, all that long way in an extremity of hot weather; although it was not worth ten shillings, when he had it at home.

(Ibid.)

In addition, the sailors in warships received prize money, a share of the proceeds from captured enemy vessels and their cargoes. But the division of spoils between the crew and the officers and the monarch was usually unfair. When the *Madre de Dios* was captured in 1592, crammed full of diamonds, pearls, rubies and other precious stones, which were worth hundreds of thousands of pounds, Queen Elizabeth I allowed the sailors only £1 each as their share of prize money. But on this occasion at least the sailors were not robbed of their just reward, for they broke into the cargo before the Queen's officers could arrive at the port, and went ashore with pockets stuffed full of jewels. One sailor admitted that he had stolen 1 800 diamonds and 300 rubies, which he sold for £130.

Another feature which made service aboard Royal ships generally unpopular was the harsh discipline. Punishments were extremely severe, as the code of naval discipline promulgated by Henry VIII in about 1530 shows.

> If any man kill another within the ship, he that doeth the deed shall be bound quick[3] to the dead man, and so be cast into the sea. . . .
> If any man draw a weapon within the ship to strike his captain, he shall lose his right hand. . . .
> If any man within the ship do sleep his watch . . . the fourth time . . . he shall be hanged on the bowsprit end of the ship in a basket, with a can of beer, a loaf of bread, and a sharp knife, [and] choose to hang there till he starve or cut himself into the sea. . . .
> If any man within the ship be a drunkard, not being content with the victuals of the ship . . . the captain shall imprison him in the bilboes[4] while he think him duly punished that so offendeth.
>
> (Orders to be used in the King's Majesty's Navy by the Sea, in H. W. Hodges and E. A. Hughes, editors: *Select Naval Documents*, Cambridge University Press, 1922)

Although there were always a certain number of volunteers aboard Royal ships, particularly when the security of the country was threatened, the Navy was unpopular with seamen because of the low pay, the savage punishments, the bad food and the generally over-crowded conditions. There were no sailors with long-service engagements in the Navy until the middle of the nineteenth century. But

[3] Alive.
[4] An iron bar with shackles which fastened round the prisoner's ankles; the maritime equivalent of the stocks.

from the earliest times, the monarch had had the traditional right to impress[5] seamen to serve in Royal ships. In times of need justices of the peace and other local authorities were given the power to seize seamen and put them aboard Royal vessels. In 1542, for example, the Lord Admiral ordered a press of men for the ships acting as a convoy to merchant vessels in the wine trade.

> Whereas dyvers of the marchauntes of Hampton and Poole are now in redines for the Sowthe and lack of marryners, this shalbe to wyll you to make for theym a commyssyon . . . to take upp so many marryners as they shall neede, to be taken at Lyme, and from thence west warde.
> (Order by the Lord Admiral to press seamen for the 'voyage de conserve' of the wine fleet, in R. G. Marsden, editor: *Documents relating to Law and Custom of the Sea*, Navy Records Society, Vol. 1, 1915)

Bargemen and watermen on the Thames were frequent victims of the press officers. They became so skilful at evading service that a law had to be passed in 1555 under which they could be banned from the Thames for a year and a day—if they were ever caught.

[5] Imprest money was paid to sailors as an advance of wages. The word gradually became corrupted into 'press', as the element of compulsion increased with the growth in the size of the Navy, and the need for more men, in succeeding centuries.

De Jongh: Watermen at work on the Thames below the old, stone London Bridge.
Greater London Council

Seamen were much more eager to serve in privateers than in Royal ships. These privateers were privately owned, armed ships which had been given authority by the monarch to seize enemy vessels in time of war, or to take reprisals against the shipping of some foreign nation for some harm done by that country in times of peace, such as seizing their cargoes or their vessels. The first letters of marque—the privateer's Royal licence—were issued in the thirteenth century and the last in the middle of the nineteenth century.

> Their Majesties be pleased, and by the authoritie hereof gyve full power and licence to all and singular their subjectes of al sortes degres and conditions that they and every of them maye . . . prepare and esquippe to the seas such and so many shippes and vessels, furnyshed for the warre, to be used and imployed agaynst their Graces sayd enemyes, as they shal thinke convenient for their advauntage and the annoiaunce of their Majesties' sayd enemyes.
>
> ('Proclamation licensing all subjects of the King and Queen to set forth ships against their enemies', 1557, in Marsden, op. cit.)

Normally the monarch took a fifth of the prize and the Lord Admiral a tenth. The rest was split into three, to be divided equally among the owners of the vessels, the victuallers who provisioned it, and the crew.

Service aboard merchant ships was also more popular than was that in Royal ships. Discipline was less harsh, the adventures were no less, the pay was also higher, and there was a good chance of making extra money. It was common practice to allow merchant seamen to indulge in private trading ventures of their own, by bringing back gold, coins, jewels, silks or porcelain from foreign countries and selling them at a profit on their return to England.

But it is impossible to make a really firm distinction between the different kinds of ships and voyages in early times: there was frequently a great mixture of motives on many of the longer journeys. Voyages of discovery were combined with acts of war and privateering. Merchants sailed side by side with discoverers. Naval captains, if not the crews, indulged in private trading ventures. Queen Elizabeth I owned ships which were engaged in the slave trade; the vast majority of English ships which defeated the Spanish Armada were armed merchant vessels.

So these small ships set out from English ports on their voyages into strange, distant seas, the crews never knowing whether the end would be capture, injury, death, or riches, honour and glory. The first really major voyage of discovery by native-born Englishmen was made in 1553 by Sir Hugh Willoughby and Richard Chancellor in search of the north-east passage to Cathay, or China.[6] At a cost of £6 000 three ships were built and fitted out: the flagship, the *Bona Esperanza* of 120 tons, the *Edward Bonaventure*, of 160 tons, and the *Bona Confidentia*, of 90 tons. In building the vessels the shipwrights took special precautions against the shipworm.[7]

> For they had heard that in certaine parts of the Ocean, a kind of wormes is bredde, which many time pearceth and eateth through the strongest oake that is: and therefore that the Mariners . . . in this voyage might bee free and safe from this danger, they cover a piece of the keele of the shippe with thinne sheetes of lead.
>
> (Clement Adams, op. cit.)

Enough food was taken aboard for a voyage of eighteen months. When all the other preparations had been made

> they departed with the turning of the water, and sailing easily, came first to Greenewich . . . (where the Court then lay) presently upon the newes thereof, the Courtiers came running out, and the common people flockt together, standing very thicke upon the shoare . . . the Mariners, they shouted in such sort, that the skie rang againe with the noyse thereof. One stoode in the poope of the ship, and by his gesture bids farewell to his friends in the best maner he coulde.
>
> (Ibid.)

After sailing round the coast to Harwich they waited for a good wind, and then set sail,

> and committed themselves to the sea, giving their last adieu to their native country, which they knewe not whether they should ever returne to see againe or not. Many of them looked oftentimes backe, and could not refraine from teares, considering into what hazards they were to fall.
>
> (Ibid.)

It was not long before these hazards appeared. After they had been sailing for several weeks, and had arrived off the coast of Norway, Sir Hugh Willoughby summoned the other captains to his ship and told them that if they were split up by a storm, each ship should make for

[6] The route, through the Arctic, and round the north coast of Asia to the Pacific, was not found until 1879 by a Swedish explorer.

[7] The shipworm, seaworm or teredo is not a worm but a specialised bivalve mollusc which bores into wood, leaving large holes.

Vardö, a port on an island off the Norwegian coast, and wait for the others to arrive.

> The very same day in the afternoone, about four of the clocke, so great a tempest suddenly arose, and the Seas were so outragious, that the ships could not keepe their intended course, but some were perforce driven one way, and some another way, to their great perill and hazard: The Generall with his lowdest voyce cried out to Richard Chanceler, and earnestly requested him not to goe farre from him.... But the said Admirall (I knowe not by what means) bearing all his sailes, was caried away with so great force and swiftnesse, that not long after hee was quite out of sight, and the third ship also with the same storme and like rage was dispersed and lost us.
>
> (Ibid.)

Only Chancellor in the *Edward Bonaventure* ever reached Vardö; the other two ships arrived in Lapland, where Sir Hugh Willoughby perished from frostbite. After waiting at the rendezvous in vain, Chancellor sailed on alone. Eventually he reached the White Sea, to the north of Russia, and travelled overland to Moscow, to negotiate a trade pact with the Tsar, Ivan the Terrible, before he returned to England. But Chancellor himself did not survive for long. Two years later he went on a second voyage to Russia, but in November 1556 was drowned after his ship foundered off Aberdeenshire.

Sailors on other voyages suffered fates almost equally harsh. One young man, Job Hortop, who was impressed to serve on a Royal ship, left England in 1567 and did not return to his native country again for twenty-two years, when he wrote a book describing his adventures and misfortunes. The vessels were engaged in the slave trade from the coasts of West Africa to the West Indies. They went first to Cape Verde, in Senegal.

> There we anchored, took our boats, and set soldiers on shore. Our General was the first that leapt on land; and with him, Captain Dudley.
>
> There, we took certain Negroes; but not without damage to ourselves; for our General, Captain Dudley, and eight others of our company were hurt with poisoned arrows.
>
> About nine days after, the eight that were wounded died. Our general was taught by a Negro, to draw the poison out of his wound, with a clove of garlic; whereby he was cured.
>
> From thence, we went to Sierra Leone, where be monstrous fishes, called sharks, which will devour men....
>
> The Captain and soldiers went up into the river called Taggarin, to take a town of Negroes: where he found three Kings of that country, with

De Bry: Francis Drake landing on the shore, not far from the river Plate in
South America.

50 000 Negroes, besieging the same town; which they could not take, in
many years before, when they had warred with it.

Our General made a breach, entered, and valiantly took the town. . . .

We took, and carried from thence, for traffic in the West Indies, 500
Negroes.

('The Rare Travailes of Job Hortop', London, 1591, reprinted in
E. Arber, editor: *An English Garner*, London, 1903)

After his ship had been forced to take refuge in a Mexican harbour
because of a storm, Hortop landed and was captured by the Spanish.
He was taken to Spain and forced to serve as an oarsman in the
Spanish galleys for many years, reaching England again only in 1590.

Many of the sailors and captains who were later to make England a great naval power served their apprenticeship in these early voyages. Francis Drake who commanded one of the other five ships on the same voyage, succeeded in escaping and sailing the *Judith* back to England. He made three more voyages to the West Indies, all of which were more successful. Then in 1577 he assembled a fleet of five ships for a venture that no Englishman had ever undertaken before. The ships were the *Pelican*, 100 tons; the *Elizabeth*, 80 tons; the *Marigold*, 30 tons; the *Swan*, 50 tons; and the *Christopher*, 15 tons.

These ships he manned with one hundred and sixty-four able and sufficient men, and furnished them also with such plentiful provision of all things necessary, as so long and dangerous a voyage did seem to require.... Neither had he omitted to make provision also for ornament and delight, carrying to this purpose with him expert musicians, rich furniture (all the vessels for his table, yea, many belonging even to the cook-room, being of pure silver) and divers shows of all sorts of curious workmanship, whereby the civility and magnificence of his native country might, amongst all nations whithersoever he should come, be more admired.

Being thus appointed, we set sail out of the Sound of Plymouth about five o'clock in the afternoon, November 15, of the same year, 1577....

(Francis Fletcher: *The World Encompassed by Sir F. Drake*, London, 1628, reprinted in David Laing Purves, editor: *The English Circumnavigators*, London, 1874)

Two of the ships were abandoned during the voyage; another with its crew of twenty-eight sank during a storm; the fourth ship gave up and returned to England. But Drake sailed on in his flagship, the *Pelican*, which was renamed the *Golden Hind* during the voyage. Just over two years and ten months later, he returned to Plymouth in triumph, having become the first Englishman to sail right round the world. The following year Queen Elizabeth I went aboard the *Golden Hind* at Deptford and knighted him. The voyage, which was partly an act of war against Spain—then the foremost maritime Power—and partly privateering, was extremely profitable. Drake captured so much treasure that investors in his expedition received £47 for every pound they had staked.

His success encouraged many others to try their luck too, including Thomas Cavendish of Trimley St Martin, near Ipswich, Suffolk, who became the second Englishman to sail round the world. On 21st July 1586 his three ships—the *Desire* of 140 tons, the *Content*, 60 tons, and the *Hugh Gallant*, 40 tons—with a total of 125 sailors aboard, set sail

De Bry: Early British explorers attacked by mythological sea lions and natives with bows and arrows.

British Museum

from Plymouth. By 5th August they had reached the Canary Islands, and then they sailed

> to the coast of Guinea unto a harbour called Sierra Leone: where, having conference with the negroes, we fell at variance; so that three score of our men went on shore, and drave them from their town, sacked their houses and burnt their dwellings. . . .
>
> Thus we sailed forth, until the 25th of October, at which time we came to the continent of Brazil. . . . On the 9th day (of November) died one Robert Smith of the disease called scorbuto;[8] which is an infection of the blood and the liver. . . .
>
> On the 5th December, died one Robert Tates of the disease aforesaid. So coasting along till the 16th of this month, we discovered an harbour which we named Port of *Desire*, according to our ship's name; being

[8] Scurvy.

almost as big as the harbour of Plymouth. In this place we had gulls, puets,[9] penguins, and seals in abundance, to all our comforts and great refreshing. . . .

> (*The worthy and famous Voyage of Master Thomas Cavendish, made round about the Globe of the Earth*, n.d., reprinted in E. Arber, op. cit.)

After sailing through the Straits of Magellan, at the southern tip of South America, they continued northward, along the coasts of Chile and Peru, until they reached the port of Acapulco in Mexico.

> We found a ship laden with cocoa, a fruit like almonds much esteemed in those parts: and taking the spoil thereof, we set the ship and the town on fire for company. . . .
> The 4th day of August, we departed from this place; and coming forth, we took a she tortoise which had about four hundred and odd eggs in her; which eggs we eat, and found them to be good meat.

> (Ibid.)

They sailed on northward, and off the Cape of California they spotted a Spanish ship of 700 tons, the *Great Saint Anna*.

> We chased her until noon; so fetching her up, we gave them fight to the loss of twelve or fourteen of their men, and the spoil and hurt of many more: whereupon at last they yielded unto us. In this conflict, we lost only two of our men.
> So on the 6th of the said November, we went into the Port of Agua Secura; where we anchored, and put nine score prisoners on land: and ransacking the great ship, we laded our own two ships with forty tons of the chiefest merchandise, and burnt all the rest, as well as the ship and goods to the quantity of 600 tons of rich merchandise: because we were not able to bring it away.

> (Ibid.)

They then sailed across the Pacific to the Philippines, through the islands of Indonesia, and on to the Cape of Good Hope, which they reached on 19th May 1588. By 7th June they had reached the island of St Helena. They passed the Azores in August and set course for home, making for the Lizard in Cornwall. On the last night

> We had as terrible a night as ever men endured. For all our sails were blown quite away, but making as good shift as we could with certain old

[9] Lapwings.

sails we had within board: on the next morning, being the 10th of September, 1588, like wearied men, through the favour of the Almighty, we got into Plymouth; where the townsmen received us with all humanity.

In this voyage, we burnt twenty sails of Spanish ships, besides divers of their towns and villages.

(Ibid.)

It was exploits such as these which gave British seamen the skills, experience and confidence to defeat the Spanish Armada. Cavendish arrived home a few months too late to take part, but he heard the news from a Dutch ship when he was still a week out from Plymouth.

The vast majority of the 200 or so English ships involved in the defeat of the Spanish Armada were merchantmen—perhaps 150 or 160. But it was the English warships, which were longer, lower in the water and swifter than either the merchantmen or the Spanish galleons, which were mainly responsible for the English victory. After a week-long battle in the English Channel (July–August 1588) the Spanish were defeated off the port of Gravelines, in northern France. The remainder of the invasion fleet sailed away, hoping to escape to their home ports by sailing round the north of Scotland, but many of them were wrecked in storms on the way.

But the British sailors who made this victory possible got little reward when they returned to shore. Their plight was so desperate that Charles Howard, later first Earl of Nottingham, who commanded the English fleet, felt compelled to write the following letter of protest to Lord Burghley, Queen Elizabeth's chief Minister:

My Good Lord:—Sickness and mortality begins wonderfully to grow amongst us; and it is a most pitiful sight to see here at Margate, how the men, having no place to receive them into here, die in the streets. I am driven myself, of force, to come a-land, to see them bestowed in some lodging; and the best I can get is barns and such outhouses.

The *Elizabeth Jonas,* which hath done as well as ever any ship did in any service, hath had a great infection in her from the beginning, so as of the 500 men which she carried out, by the time we had been in Plymouth three weeks or a month, there were dead of them 200 and above. . . .

It is like enough that the like infection will grow throughout the most part of our fleet; for they have been so long at sea and have so little shift of apparel, and so few places to provide them of such wants, and no money wherewith to buy it, for some have been—yes, the most part—these eight months at sea.

(State Papers, Domestic, Elizabeth, reprinted in
Hodges and Hughes, op. cit.)

2

During Tudor times few improvements were made in the living or working conditions of sailors. More than any other class of the population, sailors faced greater risks of death or injury, whether they were serving in a Royal ship or a merchant ship, in peace or in war. But many of those men who had been wounded in saving the country from the Spanish Armada were given in return only a licence to beg.

In 1590 Sir John Hawkins established the Chatham Chest which provided small grants of money to disabled sailors. From 1626 all sailors were obliged to contribute 6*d* a month out of their wages. Even though the chest was locked with five separate keys, it was continually raided by dishonest officials and administrators, and the sailors did not benefit very much. In a belated fit of conscience a law was passed in 1593 under which disabled sailors could be given a small pension of up to £10 a year.

Everie Parishe within this Realme of Englande and Wales shalbe charged to pay weekelye such a Some of Money towarde the Reliefe of

The old Chatham Chest with five locks, still preserved at the National Maritime Museum, Greenwich.

National Maritime Museum

sicke hurt and maymed Souldiors and Marriners . . . havinge ben pressed and in paye for her Majesties Service. . . .

('An Acte for Relief of Souldiors', in *The Statutes of the Realm*, London, Vol. 4., 1819)

Apart from these measures there were few other improvements. Hammocks were introduced in some ships in 1586. Pay in Royal ships had been increased from 6s. 8d. to 10s. a month in the previous year, but most of the benefit was soon cancelled out by inflation. The causes of the sailors' subsequent complaints through the centuries were already well established: bad food, short rations, unhealthy conditions, overdue pay, and impressment. When conditions became intolerable, their ultimate sanction was mutiny. In 1586 sailors in one of the ships in Drake's expedition to Cadiz refused to go on and turned the helm back to England. They wrote to their captain:

Captayne Marchaunt . . . Wee . . . desyre that, as you are a man and beare the name of a captayne over us, so to weighe of us like men, and lett us not be spoyled for wante of foode, for our allowauance is so smale we are not able to lyve any longer of it; . . . for what is a piece of Beefe of halfe a pounde amonge foure men to dynner of half a drye Stockfishe[10] for foure dayes in the weeke, and nothing elles to help withall—yea, wee have helpe, a little Beveredge worse than the pompe water. Wee were preste by her Majesties presse to have her allowaunce, and not to be thus dealt withall, you make no men of us, but beastes. . . .

(Add MSS 12, 505, f. 241, British Museum, quoted in Peter Kemp: *The British Sailor*, Dent, 1971)

The demand that sailors should be treated like men, not beasts, was one that was to echo and re-echo through the following centuries.

3

The British developed late as a maritime power. In the fifteenth century the Portuguese led the way, introducing the fast, ocean-going sailing-ship, the caravel; pioneering navigation by the stars; mapping the coastlines and charting the new sea routes. After their discoverers

[10] Fish dried in the sun to preserve it.

had edged along the western coasts of Africa, Vasco da Gama successfully rounded the Cape of Good Hope for the first time and sailed on to India, which he reached in 1498. Meanwhile the Spanish—the other great maritime nation at that time—had been searching for new routes to the East by sailing westward across the Atlantic. Christopher Columbus—a Genoese in the employment of the Spanish king—set sail in three small ships in 1492. He believed that he had reached the East, but in fact he had found the way to the New World, landing in the West Indies on 12th October 1492. In 1519 Ferdinand Magellan, a Portuguese also working for the Spanish king, set out with five ships on an even more adventurous mission to sail right round the world. Magellan himself was killed in the Philippines, but one of the ships, the *Victoria*, returned in 1522, becoming the first ship ever to circumnavigate the globe. Other Spanish galleons followed the same routes that these men had pioneered, sailing to the West Indies, to Mexico, and to South America, and exploiting the huge deposits of gold and silver there, which made Spain the richest and most powerful country in the world for much of the sixteenth century.

By comparison British achievements in the first half of the century were small, though some of the foundations for Britain's later ascendancy as a maritime Power were being laid. Henry VIII developed the Royal dockyards at Portsmouth, Woolwich and Deptford into some of the finest in Europe; and he built the first real battleship, the *Henry Grace à Dieu*, or *Great Harry*, in 1514. Previously warships had been used as floating platforms for soldiers—who then outnumbered the sailors on a ship—to attack enemy vessels by boarding and capturing them. There were high castles, fore and aft, which protected the soldiers, and small breech-loading guns, which were used to fire down on the enemy's decks before the soldiers went aboard. Henry introduced much larger muzzle-loading guns, which were so powerful that they could sink another vessel. The castles began to disappear—though the name remains to this day in 'fo'c's'le' (or forecastle)—and the guns were fired through ports in the gun-deck. This revolutionized the whole concept of naval warfare, by making it possible to have a longer-range shooting match between naval gunners instead of a hand-to-hand battle between soldiers. The new warships were slimmer and faster than their predecessors, too, having a keel about three times as long as the beam, instead of only twice as long as in the old 'round' ships.

Developments in British merchant shipping came later than in naval ships. The Cabots, John and his son Sebastian, Italian by race, were responsible for exploring and developing the northern sea routes, while they were in English employ. Their work bore fruit in the second half of the sixteenth century with the development of the Newfoundland fisheries and the establishment of the Company of Merchant Adventurers to trade with Russia. The great growth in the coal-carrying trade from Newcastle to London also provided a pool of experienced seamen who could be pressed into service in the Royal ships when the need arose.

The defeat of the Spanish Armada was a great turning-point in maritime power. It marked the beginning of the end for Spain as a great nation, and the rise of England towards the ascendancy which she was to retain for so many centuries.

4

1492–3	Columbus crosses Atlantic and reaches West Indies
1497–8	John Cabot's voyage to Newfoundland
1497–9	Vasco da Gama's voyage to India
1514	The *Great Harry*, the first real battleship
1519–22	Magellan's voyage round the world
1553	Willoughby's and Chancellor's voyage in search of the North-East Passage
1577–80	Drake becomes first Englishman to sail round the world
1585	Pay in Royal ships increased from 6s. 8d. to 10s. a month
1586	Hammocks introduced
1586–8	Cavendish's voyage round the world
1588	Defeat of the Spanish Armada
1590	Contributions to the Chatham Chest begin

For Further Reading
Richard Hakluyt: *Voyages and Documents*, selected and introduced by Janet Hampden, World's Classics, Oxford University Press, 1958; edited by Jack Beeching, Penguin Books, 1972

Part Two

East Indiamen and Pirates

1

During the seventeenth century there was a great increase in the size of the merchant fleet; the total tonnage rose from an estimated 67 000 in 1582 to 323 000 in 1702. From its small beginnings in coastal fishing and cross-Channel trade, the merchant service became one of the main supports of the economy. As English trade expanded merchant ships began to make regular voyages to the most distant parts of the world. Successive governments deliberately encouraged the expansion of this fast-growing industry by passing Navigation Acts, the first main one in 1651 during the Commonwealth and the second in 1660 under Charles II.

> For the Increase of Shipping, and Encouragement of the Navigation of this Nation, . . . Be it enacted . . . from and after the First Day of December One thousand six hundred and sixty . . . no Goods or Commodities whatsoever shall be imported into, or exported out of any Lands, Islands, Plantations, or Territories to his Majesty belonging . . . but in such Ships or Vessels as do truly and without Fraud belong only to the People of *England* or *Ireland*, Dominion of *Wales*, or Town of *Berwick-upon-Tweed* . . . and whereof the Master and three Fourths of the Mariners at least are *English*; under the Penalty of the Forfeiture and Loss of all the Goods and Commodities . . . as also of the Ship or Vessel. . . .
> ('An Act for the encouraging and increasing of Shipping and Navigation', in *A Collection of the Statutes*, op. cit.)

The growth of shipping and trade brought about a great expansion of the major ports, such as Bristol and Liverpool, with the building and repairing of ships, the victualling and warehousing, the loading and unloading. Above all, London grew in size and population: it is

Edward Barlow's drawing of The *Experiment* 'having stress of weather in the year 1671'.

National Maritime Museum

estimated by Ralph Davis that possibly more than one in four of all the inhabitants of the capital in 1700 were dependent in some way on the port of London.

One young lad who was attracted by all the bustling activity of the port of London was Edward Barlow, who first went to sea in 1659. Fortunately for us, he kept a lengthy journal, illustrated by himself, of his experiences: it is one of the best accounts of a sailor's life that has ever been written. Barlow was born at Prestwich, near Manchester, in 1642, the son of a poor farm labourer, who had five other children. After working on a farm for a time, he went off to London at the age of fifteen to see the world and to make his fortune. He worked in his uncle's tavern at Southwark before he signed on as an apprentice to the master's mate in H.M.S. *Naseby* at the age of seventeen.

> That night I was put into a cabin to sleep, a thing much like to some gentleman's dog-kennel, for I was forced to creep in upon all fours. . . .
> The morning being come, I got up and went about the ship to look about me, and wondered to see such a huge baulk of timber and plank joined together by many a great iron bolt . . . so that I judged it to be a seven years' work to build such a one. . . .
> (Basil Lubbock, editor: *Barlow's Journal of his Life at Sea in King's Ships, East and West Indiamen and other merchantmen from 1659 to 1703*, Hurst and Blackett, 1934)

They had not been long at sea when their food and drink began to run out, so that they had to get supplies from the land.

> And now our provisions began to run short and our beer was almost done, so we were put to shorter allowance, for what four men had before must now serve six men; and we had some of their country bread, which was black as bean bread, and some of their beer, which was as strong of smell as a thing that had hanged in the chimney seven years. . . . After about seven or eight days' sail we arrived upon the coast of England, but it being bad weather and dark some of our ships ran into danger near to Yarmouth sands. One frigate called the *Newcastle* lost her rudder, but no great harm happened, though it was very much wind.
> (Ibid.)

Although he first went to sea in a warship, Barlow spent most of his working life in the merchant service. From 1662 to 1663, he made a voyage in the *Queen Catherine* from Gravesend to Rio de Janeiro, calling at Madeira to pick up a cargo of wine and bringing back sugar from Brazil. He preferred life with the merchant service on the whole, but he found that it could have its unpleasant aspects, too.

> We were forced to go to a quart of water for a man a day, our water growing short and the rain water was not good to keep. And having gained not half our passage to the place where we were bound, this went very hard with us, being just under the sun and the weather exceeding hot. Neither had we better allowance of victuals, having but five pounds of bread for one man for seven days, with a little dry stockfish and two spoonfuls of oil for four days in a week, and the other three a little salt beef and a few peas, or a little old musty rice, faring as hard as though we had been in a King's ship and many times harder. Merchants and owners of ships in England are grown to such a pass nowadays that it is better sailing with any other nation; for when they send a ship out for a voyage they will put no more victuals or drink in the ship than will just serve so many days, and if they have to be a little longer in their passage and meet with cross winds, then the poor men's bellies must be pinched for it, and be put to shorter allowance.
>
> (Ibid.)

In view of these harsh conditions it might be wondered why Barlow continued to go to sea for so many years. One of the reasons was that when he was paid off he often received £20 or so, all in one lump sum, which was a small fortune in those days. With care it was enough to live fairly comfortably on the land for several months, and to fit himself out with new suits of clothes, and to help his relatives with money.

The other reason was his continuing desire to see the world, as he himself explained, when he decided to sail on the maiden voyage of the East India Company's *Experiment*.

> So continuing on shore at London three or four months, intending my next voyage to go for the East Indias, for I still had a mind to see strange countries; and staying for a ship which I had a mind to go in, which was then building at Blackwall, but was not quite built, at last she was finished and launched; and being rigged, I shipped myself at the East India House to go in her, she being bound for Surat in East India. . . .
>
> The goods which we took in were lead and copper and alum, and broad-cloths of red and green colour for the most part, and some other small commodities.
>
> And two or three days after, I came up to London to fetch my chest and clothes on board . . . and not long afterwards . . . we weighed our anchors with two ships more, the one called the *Loyal Subject* and the other the *Hannibal* and set sail from Gravesend.
>
> (Ibid.)

The ship called at the Cape Verde Islands for fresh provisions, and then sailed on round the Cape and up through the Mozambique Channel, where it reprovisioned at Johanna Island. The Indian coast was sighted in September, and for several months *Experiment* sailed along the coasts, unloading its cargo and loading pepper for the return journey. In January 1671 it set sail for home again, carrying in addition to its valuable cargo some spotted deer, a gift from a Company official to Charles II. The vessel (and the deer, which were taken to St James's Park) reached London safely about six months later, after encountering a violent storm which almost wrecked it. Barlow signed on in the same ship for its next voyage to Java, China and Japan.

The heavily armed East Indiamen, which were among the few merchant vessels to rival warships in size and armaments, were the pride of the mercantile marine for many years. The pay was somewhat higher than in other merchant ships, though, as was general then, deductions were made from the seamen's wages if the cargo was damaged or lost. Pensions, however, were granted to the widows of long-serving seamen who died in the company's service, and compensation was paid to men who were injured in defending their ship. But the food—hard ship's biscuit and rotten, salted meat—could sometimes be as bad as in any naval vessel, as Barlow found on his second voyage in the *Experiment*. Discipline, too, could be harsh on East Indiamen, where flogging was not unknown, as it was also on the slave traders from Liverpool.

Willaerts: A lively scene showing the departure of an East Indiaman.
National Maritime Museum

But no master of any merchant ship could afford to be as despotic as a naval captain, for they could be sued, and sometimes were, on their return to England, and made to pay damages. Nevertheless, some form of physical punishment was the commonly accepted method of maintaining discipline on merchant vessels. Captain Thomas Gullock testified at a trial at the Old Bailey in 1700 that he had beaten some of the members of his crew, who had subsequently mutinied, and left him, other members of the crew and some passengers on a small island.

> As for Chastisement, he did acknowledge that Ham, Edgell and Wetherell had been punished: Edgell because that he being a Quarter-master . . . did break open a Box and stole about a dozen pound of white Suger . . . Edward Ham . . . because . . . upon a complaint of the copper-ishness of the Pease, the Captain himself went into the Cook-room, and took off the sides of the Copper a great quantity of Verdigreese,[1] for which the Captain beat him with a Japan cane. . . . And Wetherell was beaten for striking the Boatswain of the Ship. And if Correction in such Cases be not used aboard Ships, no order can be maintain'd, but all would run into Confusion.
>
> (Anon: *A True Relation of a most Horrid Conspiracy and Running away with the Ship Adventure*, London, 1700)

But punishments of the crews of merchant ships were not always as mild as this. There is enough evidence from obviously fair-minded sailors and observers to show that a number of captains were deliberately cruel or sadistic.

> The other master I knew . . . would in a fit of the spleen fling a chip, or any other insignificant trifle, overboard, and make his men hoist out the boat and row half a mile after it; in the meantime he would make what sail he could, and keep a-head of them, making them row five or six hours after him, and a little before night lie by and take them up.
>
> (Thomas Phillips: *A Journal of a Voyage made in the Hannibal of London Ann. 1693, 1694 . . . to Barbadoes*, London, 1732)

Examples of far crueller treatment can be found right up to the nineteenth century. Food has always been such an important factor in maritime affairs that it was often the cook who suffered most. Silas Told, who first went to sea in 1725, was appalled by the brutality of

---

[1] This green rust from copper was a common cause of food-poisoning. For a similar example in the galley of a mail packet over a hundred years later see page 59.

one master of a merchant vessel under whom he had the misfortune to serve.

A second circumstance which happened on board our ship, was the Captain's inhuman cruelty to the ship's cook. The poor man had nothing but green wood to make his furnace boil with, on which account it was impossible for him to get the food ready in time. For this the Captain horsewhipped him, and stabbed him in the face, so that the poor man's life was grievously burdensome to him. Indeed he oftentimes hinted that he would throw himself overboard; but we endeavoured to dissuade him from it.

(Silas Told: *The Life of Mr. Silas Told written by himself [1776]*, London, 2nd. ed., 1954)

Such actions have to be seen in the context of the times, when servants on land were commonly beaten by their employers, and vagrants were whipped until their backs were bloody. And there is also possibly a tendency for us to hear more about the bad captains than the good. But there is little doubt that the merchant seaman's life was not one of the easiest. Under some captains the crews must have been constantly on the verge of mutiny, which one final injustice could easily provoke. This happened on a Newcastle collier, with disastrous results for all aboard, after the master had refused to let the men have the butter to which they were entitled. He ordered the crew to trim the main sail

but his men answer'd unanimously, *that not one of them would touch a rope till the firkin[2] of butter was brought to the mast.* He began to expostulate with them, but to no purpose, and seeing the ship drive near the land with all sails slack, he promised them they should have it as soon as the sails were trimm'd, and the ship had gathered way; the men reply'd, *that seeing was believing*; whereupon, finding there was no other remedy, he ran down to his cabin to fetch the butter, and laid it at the mast; then the men went to work, but too late, for e'er the sails could be hal'd about and fill'd, the ship struck upon the sand, and never came off again.

(Thomas Phillips, op. cit.)

In addition to the risk of mutiny aboard, there was the ever-present danger of being attacked by pirates, who lurked near every coast and port and in the English Channel. Few merchant seamen were lucky enough to escape one encounter with pirates or privateers at some time in their career.

[2] Small cask.

Pirates had existed from ancient times, and continued to operate in some areas, such as the China Seas, up to modern times, but they flourished greatly in the seventeenth century. From their bases in the isolated Shetlands, Hebrides and parts of southern Ireland, they preyed on merchant ships entering and leaving English ports. In the Mediterranean merchantmen were terrorized by the fierce Moorish pirates operating from the states on the Barbary coast of North Africa—Morocco, Algeria, Tunis and Tripoli. English, French and Dutch buccaneers[3]—the famous 'Brethren of the Coast'—seized shipping and raided Spanish towns in South America, from their bases in the Caribbean. The distinction between buccaneer and pirate was always somewhat fine. The buccaneers were the direct descendants of the Tudor adventurers who preyed on Spanish shipping. Contrary to popular belief, they were by no means all uneducated men. One of the most famous, William Dampier, who was born in

[3] The name came from *boucan*, a grill used for drying meat to preserve it for use in ships at sea.

Slaves aboard an Algerian pirate ship.
National Maritime Museum

Somerset in 1652, wrote a number of books, including one describing his voyage round the world, and was later given command of an Admiralty expedition to explore New Guinea and the coasts of Australia.

A number of other buccaneers achieved a respectable position in society before they died. Henry Morgan, who was born in Glamorganshire about 1635, helped to secure Jamaica for the English, was knighted by Charles II in 1674, and became lieutenant-governor of Jamaica.

The distinction between pirate and privateer was also often blurred. When pirates were captured they often claimed that they had been given letters of marque by some foreign prince or king. George Cusack, for example, a notorious pirate who was born in East Meath, Ireland, said that he had been given a commission by the French monarch, but he could not prove it, and was hanged in 1674. Service in a privateer, with its great opportunities for plunder, was often the first step towards a life of piracy. Edward Coxere, a seventeenth-century English seaman, explains how he fell into the temptation to plunder when he was serving on a Spanish privateer as a young man.

> We met another ship, a Frenchman. . . . . He was of no little worth, for he had bales of serges and ribbons. Then I began to plunder. The first which I practised was on serges, of which I got some and sent home to England. This prize we also carried into harbour. Another time we being alone at sea from the fleet in the night, we spied a great ship with which we kept company till day, that so we might take the better account of him. We found him also to be a French ship well manned and gunned. We expected to have some hot service with him, but our great guns, as we had six of brass forward, blazed at him, besides twenty-four of iron and about two hundred and twenty soldiers and seamen, that so daunted the poor Frenchmen that they soon became our prisoners. He came from Newfoundland with codfish bound home within a day or two sail of his port. This prize we turned into the old hold, with the rest.
> (E. H. W. Meyerstein, editor: *Adventures by Sea of Edward Coxere*, Oxford University Press, 1945)

The classic way of becoming a pirate was to conspire with other members of the crew to take over the ship. This is how George Cusack, who had originally been intended for the Church, started his career.

> In the year 1668, being at *Cadiz* in *Spain*, he was entertained as Gunner aboard the *Hopewell* . . . a Vessel of about 250 Tuns, and 24 Guns, bound

from Tangier to Virginia. . . . Upon the Eighth of *October* following at One of the Clock in the Morning . . . *George Cusack* with one *Richard Parslow*, one of the Mates or Pilots and several others of their Confederates, having privately armed themselves, fell upon the Watches, and by violence seized the said Captain *Lambert* . . . and several others, having first through the great Cabbin door shot the Cabbin-boy through the Thigh, and the Carpenter upon the Deck through the Buttock, whom they also wounded in the Arm. . . . At last he [Cusack] hawled out the small Boat of the Ship, and by violence forced into the Boat Captain *Lambert* with the Chief Mate, the wounded Carpenter, the Butler with three seamen more, whom he exposed to the mercy of the Ocean, denying them the Long-boat, though they begged it upon their knees. . . .

(Anon: *The Grand Pyrate: or the life and death of Capt. George Cusack the great sea-robber*, London, 1676)

Not all of the men and boys who sailed in pirate ships did so voluntarily. Sailors in captured merchant ships were often given a choice of serving with the pirates, walking the plank, or facing the hazards of the open sea in some small boat with little food or water. When a pirate ship was captured, and the men were tried, the judges usually released those who had been forced to become pirates against their will, as happened in one major trial at the Old Bailey in 1700, when 52 English, French and Dutch pirates were condemned to death.

Francis Blann, a Boy of about 13 years of age was next arraigned, but the Court considering his youth, and that he did not understand the meaning or at the least consequence of that undertaking, he was acquitted. . . .
Joseph Lasuer . . . alledged that he was taken by force from on board a Vessel laden with Corn and kept among the Pirates against his Consent, he was thereupon acquitted.

(*The Proceedings of the Court of Admiralty, by a Special Commission, being, the Tryals of all the French Pirates at the Old Baily*, London, 1700)

Piracy increased so much in the seventeenth century that a law was passed in 1700 which made it possible to try pirates anywhere in the world, instead of bringing them back to England. The penalty for piracy remained death and loss of all goods and lands, and this punishment was extended under the Act to all who aided or concealed pirates.

But the real pirates often remained unrepentant to the end, as the chaplain at Newgate prison found when William Kidd was awaiting execution. Captain Kidd, who had been sent out to Madagascar in

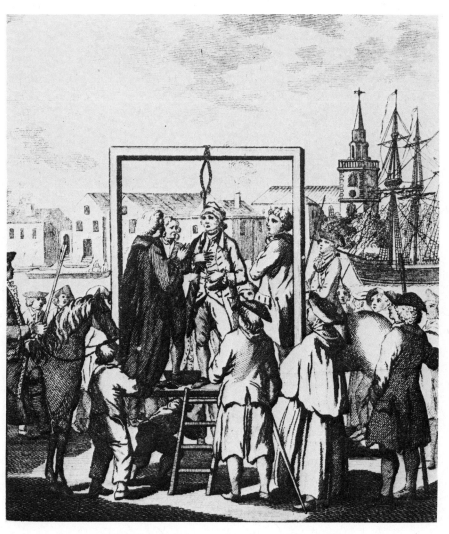

A pirate being hanged at Execution Dock.
National Maritime Museum

1696 to capture pirates, turned pirate himself and was arrested and condemned to death in 1701.

He was about 56 Years of Age, born in Scotland. I found him unwilling to confess the Crime he was convicted of, or declare any thing, otherwise than that he had been a great Offender. . . . On this Day, being the Day of

Execution, I went betimes to these Condemn'd Persons, and had them up in the Chappel, both Morning and Afternoon.... I was afraid the Hardness of Capt. Kidd's Heart, was still unmelted. I therefore apply'd my self with particular Exhortations to him, and laid the Judgments of God against impenitent and hard'ned Sinners . . . very plain before him. To all which he readily assented, and said that he truly repented of his Sins.... But having left him, to go a little before him to the Place of Execution, I found (to my unspeakable grief) when he was brought thither, that he was inflamed with Drink....

(Paul Lorrain: *The Ordinary of Newgate his account of the behaviour,*
confessions, and dying-words of Captain William Kidd,
and other Pirates, that were Executed at the Execution-Dock
in Wapping, on Friday, May 23, 1701, London, 1701)

It was not until the nineteenth century that there was enough international co-operation to end piracy at sea; by that time, too, the navies of the world were large and powerful enough to see that their Governments' decrees were carried out. But in the seventeenth century merchant ships still had to rely mainly on their own guns for protection. The bigger merchant vessels were so well armed that they stood a good chance of escaping the attentions of most pirates. But smaller ships were greatly threatened. One seaman-gunner, who served in merchant vessels during the second half of the seventeenth century, advised masters that discretion could often prove to be the better part of valour.

Though a Ship fitted for a Close Fight... and an accomplished Gunner . . . may render the most daring Attempts of an Enemy fruitless, if resolutely defended; yet a Merchant Commander is not obliged to fight, if he can with Safety shun it.... Therefore, whenever a Merchant Commander shall meet an inferiour Enemy, and, by the good Sailing of his Ship, can depart without the Hazard of a Battel, 'tis Imprudence in the Matter to venture the Owner's Ship, and the Merchant's Cargo....

(Robert Park: *The Art of Sea Fighting*, London, 1706)

The Navy did what it could to protect merchant ships, with its convoys in war and its patrols and expeditions in peace, but it was still not large enough to provide complete protection. Nevertheless, the foundations for England's future overwhelming naval power were being laid down in the seventeenth century. Charles I used ship money—the tax which helped to bring about his downfall—to build a number of ships, including the *Sovereign of the Seas* in 1637, the first three-decker with three continuous gundecks. During the Commonwealth Robert Blake, that great naval commander, brought the Navy to new heights by his victories over the Dutch, then one of the main rival maritime Powers. The expansion of naval forces, and improvements in naval administration, ships, and officers continued—not without some checks—under Charles II, James II and William III. By the end of the century a new Royal Navy had emerged, with qualified naval officers, who were beginning to make the Navy a career, instead of an occasional occupation in times of war; an administrative structure which lasted in essentials until the middle of the nineteenth century; and warships like the fast, single-decked frigate, which in their build, rigging and ordnance were distinct from merchant vessels.

One thing, however, did not change: the method by which sailors were recruited. Although there were always some volunteers, the Navy continued to rely in the main on impressment. To assemble a crew, even in times of war, sometimes took many months. This was partly because merchant seamen had become so adept at avoiding the press-gang, but even more because there simply were not enough skilled men available.

The shortage of seamen became so acute that in 1708 the Navigation Acts had to be amended to allow up to three-quarters of the crew of merchant ships to be foreigners in wartime. Service in the Navy, with its arrears of wages, poor food and harsh discipline remained generally as unpopular as it had always been.

> 15. When att any time service or action shall be commanded no man shall presume to stopp or put backward or discourage the said service and action by pretence of Arreares of Wages . . . upon pain of death. . . .
> 21. None shall presume to quarrell with his Superior officer upon pain of severe punishment nor to strike any such upon pain of death or otherwise as a Court martiall shall finde the matter to deserve. . . .
> 23. None shall quarrell or fight in the Ship nor use reproachful or provokeing speeches tending to make any quarrell or disturbance upon paine of Imprisonment and such other punishment as the Offence shall deserve and the Court martiall shall impose. . . .
>
> ('An Act for Establishing Articles and Orders for the regulating and better Government of His Majesties Navies Shipps of War and Forces by Sea', in *The Statutes of the Realm*, London, 1819)

This Act of 1661 also made desertion, spying, sedition and mutiny punishable by death, which could also be imposed for sleeping on watch or stealing from another sailor. In practice, however, the death penalty was rarely imposed, except for mutiny and sometimes for desertion. Each captain acted as his own judge and jury while he was at sea, keeping order with the traditional savage punishments of flogging and keel-hauling.

> The ducking at the main yard-arm is when a malefactor, by having a rope fastened under his arms and about his middle and under his breech, is thus hoistened up to the end of the yard and from thence is violently let fall into the sea, sometimes three several times one after another; and if the offence be very foul he is also drawn under the keel of the ship, which is termed keel raking. And whilst he is thus under water a great gun is fired right over his head, the which is done as well to astonish him so much the more with the thunder of the shot, as to give warning unto all others of the fleet to look out and to be wary by his harms. . . .
>
> As for petty pilferings and commissions of that kind, they were generally punished with the whip. . . . And commonly this execution is done upon the Monday mornings.
>
> (W. G. Perrin, editor, op. cit.)

And towards the end of the seventeenth century the Navy introduced one of the most savage punishments that man has ever devised—flogging round the fleet.[4]

2

Food, or the lack of it, has always been one of the major factors in maritime affairs, causing disease, deaths, mutinies or even in some cases, as we have already seen , shipwrecks. It was uniformly bad, and little better for the passengers in merchant ships than it was for members of the crew. One adventurous Italian who made a voyage round the world in 1693–8 found that after he had left port, and had been at sea several days, his meals consisted of:

> steaks of beef or buffalo, dry'd in the sun or wind, which are so hard that it is impossible to eat them, without they are first well beaten like stockfish; nor is there any digesting them without the help of a purge. At dinner another piece of that same sticky flesh was boil'd, without any sauce but its own hardness, and fair water. . . . On fish days the common diet was old

[4] See pages 56–7.

rank fish boil'd in fair water and salt; at noon we had ... something like kidney beans, in which there were so many maggots, that they swam at the top of the broth. ... Providence reliev'd us for a month with sharks ... the seamen caught, which, either boil'd or broil'd, were some comfort.

(Dr John Francis Gemelli Careri: *A Voyage round the World*, London, 1699)

Although the author of the above extract was travelling in a foreign ship, all the available evidence shows that food in English merchant ships was no better. On his second voyage in the East India Company's *Experiment*, Edward Barlow complained bitterly about the hard ship's biscuit, the rotten meat, and the stinking water, which made him go down with dysentery. Provisions were just as bad, if not worse, in the Navy, as Barlow found when he was serving aboard a frigate during the second Dutch war of 1665–7.

So we lay all the winter at Chatham, it being an extreme frosty and cold winter, and the river being two or three times frozen up. And we eating Peter Waren victuals,[5] as all the King's ships do when they lie in harbour, which is a little brown bread made of the worst of their wheat, and drinking a little small beer, which is as bad as water bewitched or, as the old saying is amongst us seamen,—'Take a peck of malt and heave it overboard at London Bridge and let it wash or swim down the river of Thames as low as Gravesend, and then take it up.' It would make better beer than we drunk. ...

There are no men under the sun that fare harder and get their living more hard and that are so abused on all sides as we poor seamen, without whom the land would soon be brought under subjection, for when once the naval forces are broken, England's best Walls are down.

(Edward Barlow, op. cit.)

In addition to these complaints about the poor food and the short rations, sailors in the Royal Navy had other grievances, which had already troubled them for many years and were to continue to do so for centuries.

Deptford, July 13, 1653

First, for the withholding of their wages, which they have earned with the hazard of their lives, which causes the wives and children of many of them to suffer much hardship, and disheartens them from the service.

[5] Petty warrant issued by the clerk of check to the victualler every week or every few days when a ship was in port. These two often combined with the purser to cheat the men out of their proper rations.

Secondly, for the violent pressing and carrying away those poor men whose wages is so stopped without any care taken for their distressed families in their absence. Thirdly, the bad provision is made for them at sea, being necessitated in many ships to feed upon unwholesome and stinking victuals, whereby many of them are become sick and unserviceable, and many are dead.

(George Kendal to Admiralty Commissioners in C. T. Atkinson, editor: *Letters and Papers relating to the First Dutch War, 1652–1654*, Navy Records Society, Vol. V, 1912)

Some attempts were made to improve the sailor's lot, both under the Commonwealth and when Samuel Pepys was the official mainly responsible for naval affairs. Cromwell and his generals-at-sea displayed at first a much greater concern for sailors than Charles I had done. They tried to ensure that they received their wages on time, and in 1653 their wages were increased to 24*s.* a month for an able seaman and 19*s.* for ordinary seamen. (They were not raised again for nearly 150 years!) Tarpaulin captains, who had learnt their craft the hard way, replaced the gentlemen-captains who often had little understanding of either the ships or the men they commanded. And Cromwell himself was always willing to lend a sympathetic ear to those who had suffered in the Commonwealth's service, by granting requests such as the following:

TO HIS HIGHNESS, THE LORD PROTECTOR *of the Commonwealth of England, Scotland, and Ireland.*
THE HUMBLE PETITION *of* MARGERY, *the wife of* WILLIAM BEACHAM, *mariner, Sheweth,*

That your Petitioner's husband hath been active and faithful in the wars of this Commonwealth, both by sea and land, and hath undergone many hazards by imprisonment and fights, to the endangering his life, and at last lost the use of his right arm, and is utterly disabled from future service, as doth appear from the certificate annexed; and yet he hath no more than forty shillings from Chatham by the year.

That your petitioner having only one son who is tractable to learn, and not having wherewith to bring him up, by reason of their present low state occasioned by the public service aforesaid,

Humbly prayeth—That your Highness would vouchsafe to present her said son Randolph Beacham, to be a scholar in Sutton's Hospital, called the Charter-house.

(Quoted in William Hone: The *Year Book of Daily Recreation and Information*, London, 1832)

But Cromwell was unable to provide a long-term cure, and by the time of the Restoration in 1660 wages were in arrears to a total of

£750 000 again. Samuel Pepys also had a genuine concern for the plight of seamen.

October 31, 1666
   Late to supper with my wife and brother, and then to bed. And thus ends the month with an ill aspect, the business of the Navy standing wholly still. . . . The seamen grow very rude, and every thing out of order; commanders having no power over their seamen, but the seamen do what they please. Few stay on board, but all coming running hither to towne, and nobody can with justice blame them, we owing them so much money; and their familys must starve if we do not give them money, or they procure it upon their tickets from some people that will trust them.
                    (*Diary of Samuel Pepys*, London, 1877, Vol. 4)

Pepys first became responsible for naval affairs when he was appointed Clerk of the Acts in 1660 and was finally Secretary to the Admiralty from 1673 to 1679 and again from 1684 to 1688. One of the main reasons for the sailor's hard life was the widespread corruption among officers. The Chatham Chest, despite the five keys, was regularly rifled by those in charge of it. The ship's cook could make so much money by cheating the men out of their authorized rations that the office was regularly sold, for what were then very large sums of money.

   John CURLE, 48 years, cook of the Victory, 16th July, 1608: Sayeth that he bought the place which he now holds of one Richard Lewis . . . and paid for the same the sum of £40. . . .
   And he further sayeth that he verily believeth that few cooks are placed in the navy which came fairly by their places without money paid for the same.
                    (A. P. McGowan, editor: *The Jacobean Commissions of Enquiry 1608 and 1618*, Navy Records Society, 1971)

   Some pursers cheated the men out of their wages. These were paid, not in cash, but in the form of tickets, which had to be exchanged at an office ashore. But very often the office had no money and the sailor was forced to sell his ticket—at a big discount—to whoever would buy it: an innkeeper, a ticket broker, or the ship's purser himself. Pepys tried to ensure that the seamen received their wages regularly, that food was improved, and that each ship carried a stock of slop clothing at a reasonable price. In spite of his zeal, irregularities persisted, and continued for many more years: Pepys himself made a small fortune while he was holding office.

Towards the end of the century William III, the Dutchman who ruled England jointly with his English wife, Mary, after the revolution of 1688, introduced one much-needed reform. Holland had long provided hospitals, or retirement places, for wounded or aged soldiers and sailors. William ordered that the old Tudor palace at Greenwich which was being restored, should be made into a Royal Hospital for sailors. Work on the new buildings, to the designs of Christopher Wren, was started in 1696, and the hospital was finally opened in 1705. Its work was partly financed by the seamen themselves.

> Every Seamen whatsoever, that shall serve . . . in any of his Majesty's Ships, or in any Ship or Vessel whatsoever, belonging . . . to any Subjects of England . . . shall allow Sixpence *per Mensem*, for the better Support of the said Hospital. . . .
>
> ('An Act for the Increase and Encouragement of Seamen, 1696', in *A Collection of the Statutes*, op. cit.)

Although both merchant seamen and naval ratings had to contribute 6*d*. a month, the hospital was never large enough to provide accommodation for all of those who were in need. At its peak, in the nineteenth century, the hospital accommodated over 2 800 men. For these it provided a roof over their heads, food—and pocket money of 1*s*. a week.

3

The seventeenth century was the crucial period for the development of English merchant shipping and of the Royal Navy. The two main 'nurseries' of English seamen—the Newfoundland and Icelandic fisheries, and the coastal coal-carrying trade—continued to expand at an extremely rapid rate until at least the middle of the century. But the most spectacular change was the increase in the number of larger, ocean-going vessels through the extension of trade to new areas of the world. The Levant Company, which received its charter in 1581, had a monopoly of the valuable trade with the eastern Mediterranean, bringing back cargoes of Turkish and Persian silk in exchange for woollen cloths. Its ships were large for those

Clevely: A sailing ship being built on the stocks at Deptford in the middle of the eighteenth century.

Greenwich Hospital Collection

times, ranging from about 300 to 600 tons, and heavily armed to protect themselves against the Barbary pirates. The East India Company, chartered in 1600, sent its vessels into Eastern waters to bring back pepper, spices, silk and cotton, and, from the end of the century, tea, which was then becoming a fashionable drink in Europe. At first the company built its own ships at Deptford, including several huge ships (for those times) of 1 000 tons; but the first of these, the *Trade's Increase*, launched in 1609, was wrecked on its maiden voyage, with the loss of its valuable cargo. As a result the company started to use smaller ships, and after twenty years or so, stopped building ships itself, and chartered new vessels from private owners usually for four voyages of eighteen months' duration. Most of the ships were 300 to 500 tons, —minute by present-day standards, but then among the largest ships afloat: in the middle of the century, about half of Bristol's ships were probably under 100 tons.

From about the middle of the century there was a great increase in trade with North America, where the first English settlement had been established in 1607, and with the West Indies. Tobacco was brought back from the plantations in Virginia and Maryland, and sugar from the Caribbean islands. The slave trade, from the coasts of West Africa to the West Indies, which had been started during the

Tudor period by Sir John Hawkins, continued to flourish, mainly in ships from Liverpool, Bristol and London. There was also a considerable increase in the Baltic trade of timber and corn.

This all-round increase in merchant shipping brought England into conflict with other maritime Powers, particularly the Dutch, who were then one of the most powerful. The East India Company, which had originally intended to take part in the rich trade with the East Indies, were driven out of practically the whole area by the Dutch within twenty years, and had to build up a trade with India instead. The Navigation Acts of 1651 and 1660, which restricted the carrying of English goods to English ships, were directed mainly against the Dutch. Commercial rivalry led to the First Dutch War of 1652–4. This was highly successful for the English. Contemporaries estimated that at least a thousand Dutch merchant ships were captured, probably most of them flyboats—then the most advanced European cargo ships. These cheap freighters had long keels, large holds and fewer sails, so that they could be operated with a smaller crew, which cut down on wages. A second war was fought against the Dutch from 1665 to 1667, but was much less successful. Far fewer prizes were captured, and the English suffered a humiliating defeat when the Dutch admiral de Ruyter sailed up the Medway, destroyed English warships and towed away the English flagship, the *Royal Charles*. The sounds of Dutch gunfire could be heard in London. A further war was fought against the Dutch in 1672 to 1674, but after the English revolution of 1688, when William III became king, the Dutch and the English became allies against the threatening power of France. The long period of warfare, which lasted until the Treaty of Utrecht, saw many naval engagements against the French and the Spanish, but England emerged as the main maritime Power, though the Navy was allowed to stagnate again after Walpole secured a temporary peace with France.

4

1600   East India Company chartered
1637   *Sovereign of the Seas,* first warship with three continuous gun-
       decks
1651   First main Navigation Act

1652–4 First Anglo-Dutch War
1653   Wages increased to 24s. a month for able seamen and 19s. for ordinary seamen
1660   Second Navigation Act
1665–7 Second Anglo-Dutch War
1672–4 Third Anglo-Dutch War
1673   Pepys becomes Secretary to the Admiralty
1674   Henry Morgan, buccaneer, knighted
1698   First flogging round the fleet
1701   William Kidd, pirate, executed
1705   Royal Hospital, Greenwich, opened

For Further Reading
Sir Arther Bryant: *Samuel Pepys, The Saviour of the Navy*, Cambridge University Press, 1938; Collins, 1949
Philip Gosse: *The History of Piracy*, Cassell, 1954
L. A. Wilcox: *Mr. Pepys' Navy*, Bell, 1966

Part Three

The Press-gang

1

During the eighteenth century new efforts had to be made to find sufficient seamen for the growing number of merchant ships. The problem became particularly acute in times of war, when the needs of the expanded Royal Navy also had to be met. During the War of the Spanish Succession, 1702–13, the shortage became so serious that the parish workhouses had to be scoured to find boy recruits for the merchant service.

It shall and may be lawful . . . for the Churchwardens and Overseers of the Poor . . . to bind and put out any Boy or Boys, who is, are, or shall be of the Age of Ten Years or upwards, or who is, are, or shall be chargeable, or whose Parents are or shall become chargeable to the respective Parish or Parishes wherein they inhabit, or who shall beg for Alms, to be Apprentice or Apprentices to the Sea Service to any of her Majesty's Subjects, being Masters or Owners of any Ship or Vessel . . . until such Boys shall respectively attain or come to the Age of One and Twenty Years. . . .
VIII. All . . . Masters or Owners of the Burthen of Thirty Tun to the Burthen of Fifty Tun, be obliged to take One such Apprentice; and One more for the next Fifty Tun, and One more for each and every Hundred Tun. . . .
XVI. Idle Persons, Rogues, Vagabonds, and sturdy Beggars . . . do continue to wander up and down, pilfering and begging through all Parts of this Kingdom . . . and are hereby directed to be taken up, sent, conducted and conveyed into her Majesty's Service at Sea. . . .
('An Act for the Increase of Seamen, and better Encouragement of Navigation, and Security of the Coal Trade, 1704', in *A Collection of the Statutes*, op. cit.)

The parish workhouses must have taken this opportunity to send all their unwanted pauper boys into the Merchant Navy, for only two

Britannia looks on benignly as orphan boys are enlisted in the Marine Society 'For the Service of our Country'.

British Museum

years later a new Act had to be passed permitting masters to reject any boys under thirteen and all who appeared to be sick or weak.

In 1756, at the beginning of the Seven Years' War, Jonas Hanway (reputedly the first Englishman to carry an umbrella), formed the Marine Society, which put into operation a most successful and ingenious scheme for naval recruiting. Instead of forcing orphans and pauper-boys to serve in merchant ships by law, it tried to encourage them to enter the Royal Navy direct by offering them a special bounty of a suit of clothes and a few other personal possessions. In this way society got rid of some of the burdens on the poor-rate, and the Navy got its urgently needed recruits. The Society obtained its money mainly from public subscriptions: George II gave £1 000 and the Prince of Wales £400. In just over three years nearly £20 000 was raised.

Enticing advertisements, such as the following, were inserted in the newspapers.

Notice is hereby given
THAT all STOUT LADS and BOYS, who incline to go on board HIS MAJESTY'S ships, *as servants*, with a view to learn the *duty of a seaman* . . . shall be handsomely *clothed* and provided with *bedding*, and their

charges borne down to the ports where HIS MAJESTY'S SHIPS lye, with all other proper encouragement.

(Ibid.)

When the boys had enrolled with the Society they were given the following clothes and personal possessions:

1 Felt-hat, with a cockade, and quality-binding
2 Worsted caps
1 Blue kersey-jacket, with blue horn-buttons
1 Waistcoat of blue half-thick, ditto
1 Pair of Drawers, ditto
1 Pair of canvas-trousers
2 Pair of yarn-hose
2 Pairs of shoes
2 Handkerchiefs
3 $\frac{3}{4}$ check-shirts
1 Ticken mattress
1 Ditto pillow
1 Blanket
1 Coverelet
1 Paper, containing 7 needles
                    5 Balls of worsted
                    2 Ounces of thread
1 New Testament
1 Seaman's monitor
1 Dr. Synge's Christian Knowledge
1 Knife
1 Pair of buckles
1 Pair of buttons
1 Havre-sack

(Ibid.)

Before the boys set out from the Society's office to join their ships (in a conducted party to make sure that they did not run away with all their fine new clothes) they were given a final address by the secretary or a member of the committee. It started:

My good lads, attend to what I am going to say: you are going into the wide world; and will meet with some difficulties; expect them, but be not disheartened; they will lead you to comfort and honor, if not profit and pleasure, and these cannot be obtained without labor. Some of you are relieved from great misery and wretchedness. You are now in the way of making your fortune, and I hope may share in the spoils of the enemy; but you must be contented with your wages, if it happens otherwise. . . .

(Ibid.)

When the warship returned to port and the crews were discharged the Society tried to place its boys with the master of a merchant vessel so that they would not be lost to the sea. Landsmen-volunteers were given similar quantities of clothing, though no sleeping gear was provided when a bounty of 30s. was introduced shortly after the war had begun. The Society was extremely successful in its work, particularly as it claimed to enrol only volunteers. By the time the Seven Years' War ended in 1763 over 10 000 boys and men had been recruited for the Navy, which is perhaps some measure of the even more wretched life that many people must have suffered on the land.

In spite of this new source of recruits, the Navy still had to rely mainly on its traditional methods of finding crews—the press-gang. During the second half of the eighteenth century impressment rose to a peak, as the demand for more and yet more sailors grew. As a result of the American War of Independence and the wars against the French revolutionaries, and then Napoleon, the Royal Navy expanded to an unprecedented size. (The peak was reached in 1809–10, when there were over a thousand naval ships in commission and nearly 150 000 men in the Service.)

Throughout the century various writers proposed alternatives to impressment. One suggested that a skeleton crew of 15 to 100 men should be retained in warships, instead of all the sailors being paid off at the end of each commission, and that a permanent register of seamen should be kept.

But a voluntary register of seamen had already been tried under an Act of 1696, and had soon failed; and it was still considered too expensive to maintain permanent crews on warships when they were not in commission. So, the press-gang, which has become part of the folklore of British social history, continued its operations, both on land and at sea. The easiest method was to impress seamen as they were returning home from a voyage in a merchant ship.

Although this method of impressment was the easiest, it often created friction with the masters of merchant vessels, who did not want to lose most of their most highly skilled seamen to the Navy. But an even more serious effect of this method of impressment was that the convoys of merchantmen frequently scattered to avoid the press tenders when they approached the English coasts, so that they became an easy prey for enemy privateers lurking in the Channel.

Even after the vessel had been boarded, merchant seamen sometimes managed to escape successfully, as John Nicol and William Mercer did when they returned from Lisbon in a Portuguese ship in 1792.

When we arrived at Gravesend a man-of-war's boat came on board to press any Englishmen there might be on board. . . . So we stowed ourselves away among some bags of cotton, where we were almost smothered, but could hear every word that was said. The captain told the lieutenant he had no more hands than he saw, and they were all Portuguese. The lieutenant was not very particular, and left the brig without making much search. When the boat left the vessel we crept from our hiding hole, and not long after a custom-house-officer came on board. I . . . gave the custom-house-officer half-a-guinea for the loan of his cocked hat and powdered wig; the long gilt-headed cane was included in the bargain. I got a waterman to put me on shore . . . I inquired of the waterman the way to the inn, where the coach set out from for London; I at the same time knew as well as him. I passed for a passenger. At the inn I called for a pint of wine, pens and ink, and was busy writing any nonsense that came in my head until the coach set off. All these precautions were necessary. Had the waterman suspected me to be a sailor, he would have informed the press-gang in one minute. The waiters at the inn would have done the same.

By these precautions I arrived safe in London, but did not go down to Wapping until next day, where I took up my old lodgings, still in my disguise.

(John Nicol: *The Life and Adventures of John Nicol,
Mariner*, Edinburgh, 1822)

But the press-gang is chiefly remembered for its activities on the land. The gang was led by an officer, who established his 'rendezvous', or headquarters, in some convenient tavern, where a flag was hoisted and posters were put up. The gang itself was usually composed partly of sailors and partly of local men, who were specially recruited for their toughness and strength. Then, armed with cudgels, they patrolled the streets of the town in search of any likely-looking recruits, who would be seized and dragged back by force to the rendezvous.

In the midst of this agreeable reverie, I was, when crossing Towerhill, accosted by a person in seamen's dress who tapped me on the shoulder enquiring in a familiar and technical strain 'what ship?' I assumed an air of gravity and surprise and told him I presumed he was under some mistake as I was not connected with shipping. The fellow, however, was too well acquainted with his business to be thus easily put off. He gave a whistle and in a moment I was in the hands of six or eight ruffians who I immediately dreaded and soon found to be a press gang. . . . I was immediately carried into the presence of the Lieutenant of the gang, who questioned me as to my proffession, whither I had ever been to sea, and what business had

The press gang at work in London.
National Maritime Museum

taken me to Towerhill. I made some evasive replies . . . but my hands being examined and found hard with work, and perhaps a little discoloured with tar . . . I was remanded for further examination. . . .

(M. D. Hay, editor: *Landsman Hay, The Memoirs of Robert Hay, 1789–1847*, Rupert Hart-Davis, 1953)

In theory it was only able-bodied, British-born seamen between the ages of eighteen and fifty-five who were liable to be pressed. But as the demand for men grew, not even those who were officially and legally exempt could feel safe any more. Apprentices, foreigners, the young, the old, even aldermen, shopkeepers and wealthy shipowners were forcibly seized and dragged back to the rendezvous. The gangs grabbed their men and let their superior officers, and sometimes the Admiralty, argue about the law afterwards. Seamen who had no fixed home fled inland to escape the press-gang.

His Majesty's Ship *Venerable*
in Torbay, 26 April, 1803.

Sir,

   In pursuance of your order, I went last night to Dartmouth, with the Officers and men previously directed, and made a strict search in all the Public Houses, and in every other place where the Lieutenant of the Rendezvous thought there might be a probability of success.... I am sorry to say the result of all these endeavours only produced two men; this is, I imagine, to be accounted for by the same duty having been several times performed at Dartmouth since the first breaking out of the Impress, which has made the seamen too wary to be suddenly caught; indeed I am informed that the greater part of them are retired some miles into the country, particularly at the back of Teignmouth....

Sir,

Your respectful and obedient servant,
J. C. SEARLE.
('Public Record Office, Admiralty, Captains' Letters',
quoted in Hodges and Hughes, op. cit.)

On this occasion no civilians or exempted men were picked up, as the Admiral had given secret instructions to the press officers to act with 'as much caution as possible', following a 'very unpleasant' incident at Portland, involving 'bloodshed and violent measures'. Such incidents were by no means uncommon. In the following year William Trim, a seaman of Poole, fought back against the press-gang with a red-hot poker after they had broken into his house: one of the gang stabbed his seventy-year-old father in the back, and his sister was assaulted. Angry women came to the assistance of their threatened menfolk. This happened at Sunderland in 1803, when the women of the town rose up against the press-gang. Captain Adam Mackenzie, who was in charge of all operations on Tyneside, went back into the town with all his press-gangs and a strong force of sailors. Afterwards he wrote to the Admiralty:

   The seamen all fled, but we were attacked by large Mobs, principally women, who by throwing things hurt some of the Officers, and rescued several men.
   At last the only Magistrate at home in the Town, directed the 30th Regt. to assist in keeping the peace, our own people however had conquered every difficulty without hurting anyone, and I now think the Officer and Gang may go on with their duty.
   We took twenty-two men, but found only five fit for the Service....
(Quoted in Norman McCord: 'The Impress Service in
North-East England during the Napoleonic War', in *The
Mariner's Mirror*, Vol. 54, Cambridge University Press, 1968)

Apart from its great expense, its violence, its doubtful legality, and its unpopularity with the civilian population, the press-gang was not a particularly efficient means of raising men, as some random comments by naval captains reveal.

> Blackguards.
> Sorry poor creatures that don't earn half the victuals they eat . . .
> Poor ragged souls, and very small . . .
> Twenty-six poor souls, but three of them seamen.
> Ragged and half dead.
> Landsmen, boys, incurables and cripples. Sad wretches great part of them are.
> More fit for an hospital than the sea.
> All the ragg-tagg that can be picked up.
>
> (J. R. Hutchinson: *The Press-gang Afloat and Ashore,*
> London, 1913)

But even the press-gangs were not capable of filling the warships during the Napoleonic wars. An Act passed in 1795 extended the Navy's net even further inland by making it compulsory for each county in England and Wales to supply a certain number of men for naval service. A second Quota Act, passed in the same year, imposed the same obligations on ports. Many local authorities took this opportunity to unload their criminals on the Navy, and these Lord Mayor's men, as they were called, were never very popular among professional sailors.[1] Most seaports also tried to encourage sailors to volunteer for service by offering a bounty of their own in addition to the King's bounty. In 1779, during the American War of Independence, Liverpool corporation gave a bounty of ten guineas to every able seaman and five guineas to ordinary seamen.

All these recruits—pressed men, Quota men, and sometimes even volunteers—eventually ended up in the Admiral's tender which conveyed them out to the waiting warships.

> Upon getting on board this vessel, we were ordered down in the hold, and the gratings put over us; as well as a guard of marines placed round the hatchway with their muskets loaded and fixed bayonets, as though we had been culprits of the first degree, or capital convicts. In this place we spent the day and following night huddled together, for there was not room to sit or stand separate: indeed, we were in a pitiable plight, for numbers of them were sea-sick, some retching, others were smoking,

---

[1] On the other hand, some were better-educated men, who may have been partially responsible for the Spithead and Nore mutinies.

whilst many more were so overcome by the stench, that they fainted for want of air. As soon as the officer on deck understood that the men below were overcome with foul air, he ordered the hatches to be taken off, when day-light broke in upon us; and a wretched appearance we cut, for scarcely any of us were free from filth and vermin.

> (Jack Nastyface [William Robinson]: *Nautical Economy;*
> *or Forecastle recollections of events during the last war,*
> London, 1836)

It wasn't a lack of courage, of toughness, or of patriotism that made merchant seamen reluctant to serve in warships, but simply that they had so much to lose if they were pressed. When they were taken off their homeward-bound ships they were deprived of the chance of seeing their family or wife again, after having sometimes already been absent from home for many months. There was no shore leave because of the risk of desertion. In theory, it was the duty of the press officer to see that the seamen received a ticket from the master of the merchant vessel for the wages due to him, but this duty was sometimes neglected. As a result it could be months or years before the sailor got his wages, even if he ever did. Furthermore, the pay in the Navy was still unchanged from Cromwell's time—24s. a month for able seamen and 19s. for ordinary seamen. But, even before the Napoleonic wars, the merchant seamen's wages were 25s. to 35s. a month, and, with the shortage of men, they rose to unprecedented heights during the wars. By 1800 they had reached 84s. a month in some cases, and four years later some merchant seamen were getting 126s. a month, though these were mainly foreigners, as by then most British seamen had been impressed. It is true that sailors in some ships, particularly frigates, had a chance of gaining prize money if their ship captured a foreign vessel. But this was a gamble, and for the seaman it usually amounted only to £5 or £10, though there were exceptional cases in which they received several hundred pounds. (The flag officer and the captain, however, received many thousands of pounds when a valuable prize was captured.)

Discipline, too, aboard naval ships became even harsher during the eighteenth century. Under the Admiralty regulations, first issued in 1731, a captain was only allowed to punish a sailor with up to twelve lashes of the cat-o'-nine tails. But these regulations were commonly ignored by some captains, who ordered three or four dozen lashes for laziness, drunkenness, even for laughing in the presence of an officer, or for allowing another warship to get its sails up first. But the most brutal and awesome punishment of all—flogging round the fleet—could only be ordered by a court martial for some more serious

Cruikshank: A sailor being flogged in 1825.
National Maritime Museum

offence—stealing, desertion, mutiny. The man, tied to a scaffold, was rowed from ship to ship, to be flogged by each boatswain's mate in turn until he had received the stipulated total of up to 500 lashes or more, while drummers beat the Rogue's March. The man usually died or was maimed for life.

One of our men was whipped through the fleet for stealing some dollars from a merchant ship he was assisting to bring into port. It was a dreadful sight; the unfortunate sufferer tied down on the boat, and rowed from ship to ship, getting an equal number of lashes at the side of each vessel from a fresh man. The poor wretch, to deaden his sufferings, had drunk a whole bottle of rum a little before the time of punishment. When he had only two portions to get of his punishment, the captain of the ship perceived he was tipsy, and immediately ordered the rest of the punishment to be delayed until he was sober. He was rowed back to the *Surprise*, his back swelled like a pillow, black and blue; some sheets of thick blue paper were steeped in vinegar and laid to his back. Before he seemed insensible, now his shrieks rent the air. When better he was sent to his ship, where his tortures were . . . again renewed.

(John Nicol, op. cit.)

Impressment created an inescapable trap for the Navy. Such punishments were possibly necessary to control the 'ragg-tagg' that the press-gangs brought in; but at the same time they stopped many of the more intelligent and skilled merchant seamen from volunteering to serve aboard warships. These barbaric punishments also appalled the foreigners who witnessed them. The Chinese, whom Palmerston was later to describe as 'half-civilized', were

> much alarmed at the appearance of a man-of-war ship, and they often say, 'Englishman too much cruel—too much fight.' There were some English seamen flogged for mutiny while we lay in the river. The Chinese wept like children for the men, saying, 'Hey, yaw. Englishman too much cruel,—too much flog,—too much flog.'
>
> (John Nicol, op. cit.)

2

Conditions aboard all ships at that time were harsh: Samuel Kelly describes his life aboard a postal packet at the end of the eighteenth century in the following way:

> In this ship I was stationed when at sea in the main-top,[2] and I imagine I have slept hundreds of hours in this top, even when the ship has been rolling nearly gunwale in, and often pitching with very sudden jerks against a head sea, but through mercy I was never thrown out of the top, and the pillow I made use of was a small box of gunpowder deposited there for the hankerbusses and blunderbusses[3] in case of engaging the enemy. This dangerous box, generally served as a pillow even in thunder and lightning, which is very frequent in squalls in warm climates. The greatest trouble I had in this top was attending the sails that were hoisted on a long top-gallant mast[4] full thirty feet in the hoist, and on this mast I was obliged to haul myself up by main strength, with my hands. When all the sails were set, to take in and out and send into the top, the upper sail . . . was not only a very painful and teasing employment, but also very

[2] A little platform at the top of the lower main mast, used for observation and for firing down on the decks of enemy ships with small arms.
[3] Ancient guns.
[4] The third highest mast, above the top mast and the lower mast.

dangerous, as this mast used to bend and spring like a coachman's whip. . . .

On one passage many of the crew were attacked with excruciating pains in their bowels, and I believe nearly half our men were confined to their hammocks. This disease our surgeon supposed to be the effect of poison. Accordingly the copper boilers were examined, and a quantity of verdigris was discovered on the inside of the pease copper, which the cook's mate had neglected to clean, as usual. . . .

This ship being a contract one, our provisions were of infamous quality, the beef appeared coarse, and such as is cured for negroes, the barrels of pork consisted of pigs' heads with the iron rings in the nose, pigs' feet and pigs' tails with much hair thereon. Each man had six pounds of bread and five pounds of salted meat per week, but neither beer, spirits nor candle were allowed.

(Samuel Kelly, op. cit.)

Even naval officers did not have an easy life, as one landsman (not without some connections with the Service) observed in his diary in 1781, after he had visited two warships at Leith.

Sat. June 16 I have always thought a ship with all the conveniences that can possibly be contrived a most terrible place to live in—the dirty appearance of the men in between decks—the smell of their bedding, cookery etc. is to me nauseous. The captain's apartment is the only one in which I could subsist any time. The state room, as it is called, where the Lieutenants, the Captain of Marines, Master, Surgeon, etc. keep, is no better than a kind of disagreeable coffee room, from which the adjoining cabins of these officers are only separated by canvas hangings.

(Basil Cozens-Hardy, editor: *The Diary of Sylas Neville, 1767–1788*, Oxford University Press, 1950)

Although most sailors were prepared to accept the inevitable hardships of their life, and all its attendant dangers of storms, shipwrecks, or capture by pirates or the enemy, they were no longer prepared to tolerate some of the unnecessarily harsh conditions that were imposed on them by their employers or by naval officers. As the eighteenth century drew to a close with the outbreak of the American War of Independence and the French Revolution, there was a new breath of liberty and freedom in the air, a sense that the old corruption need not last for ever more. Something of this same spirit imbued the astonishing and unprecedented naval mutinies at Spithead and the Nore, which were preceded by one of the biggest riots ever recorded by merchant seamen. The main cause on both occasions was pay.

The outbreak of the American War of Independence in 1775 caused the loss of one large market for Negro slaves and resulted in considerable unemployment among seamen in Liverpool, which was one of the main ports engaged in this unsavoury trade. Shipowners reduced the wages of seamen from 30*s.* to 20*s.* a month. This caused riots on some of the slaving ships, with seamen tearing down the rigging. The ringleaders were arrested and taken off to prison, when some two to three thousand sailors marched to the prison to rescue them, and then threatened to destroy the Exchange. The disturbance—one of the few in England in which a cannon has been used—lasted four days, before it was quelled by the military.

In contrast, the naval mutinies during the war against Revolutionary France were much more disciplined and highly organized, particularly the first one at Spithead. In April 1797 crews in sixteen ships of the Channel Fleet refused to put out to sea when ordered to do so. Instead two delegates from each ship were rowed over to the *Queen Charlotte*, where they took over the great state cabin as their headquarters. Their petition to the Admiralty of 18th April succinctly listed their grievances.

MY LORDS

We, the seamen of his majesty's navy, take the liberty of addressing your lordships in an humble petition, shewing the many hardships and oppressions we have laboured under for many years, and, which, we hope, your lordships will redress as soon as possible. . . .

The first grievance we have to complain of, is, that our wages are too low, and ought to be raised, that we might be the better able to support our wives and families in a manner comfortable. . . .

That our provisions be raised to the weight of sixteen ounces to the pound, and of a better quality. . . .

That there might be granted a sufficient quantity of vegetables, of such kind as may be the most plentiful in the ports to which we go; which we grievously complain and lay under the want of.

That your lordships will be pleased seriously to look into the state of the sick on board his majesty's ships, that they may be better attended to. . . .

That we may in somewise have grant and opportunity to taste the sweets of liberty on shore, when in any harbour, and when we have completed the duty of our ship, after our return from sea. . . .

That if any man is wounded in action, his pay may be continued till he is cured and discharged. . . .

Given on board the *Queen Charlotte*, by the delegates of the fleet, the 18th day of April, 1797.

(*The Annual Register*, 1797, quoted in G. E. Manwaring and Bonamy Dobrée: *The Floating Republic*, Penguin, 1937)

The mutiny was conducted with gentlemanly respect and decorum on both sides. The mutineers put unpopular officers and their baggage ashore, but continued to do their normal duties, maintained discipline themselves, and stressed that they would put out to sea to fight the French if it was necessary. Lord Bridport, the commander of the Channel Fleet, adopted a conciliatory line, and after some initial hesitations and blunders the Government and the Admiralty conceded most of the demands, except the request for shore leave. The wages of able seamen were raised from 24s. to 29s. 6d. a month, and those of ordinary seamen from 19s. to 23s. 6d. Within a month it was all over: the men who took part had been granted a Royal pardon, and the Admiralty promised that there would be no victimization. This promise was kept: some of the ringleaders were promoted within the year. The main reason for this surprisingly swift and moderate conclusion was the obvious justice of the men's respectful demands for these long-overdue reforms. Many of the more moderate officers probably had some sympathy with the men's aims—if not their methods—as did Lieutenant Philip Beaver, of the *Monarch.*

They have all . . . behaved with great prudence, decency and moderation . . . but are determined to have an increase of pay. . . .

As an officer, I must condemn their conduct; as a well-wisher to my country, I must regret its being so exceedingly ill-timed; but as a man, I can find many excuses for them. I could say many things to extenuate their conduct. . . .

(E. Hallam Moorhouse, editor: *Letters of the English Seamen, 1587–1808*, Chapman and Hall, 1910)

But the mutiny at the Nore, which broke out a few days before the Spithead mutiny ended, was a very different affair. The mutineers' demands were much greater: they wanted a pardon for deserters, a more equal share of prize money, and the right to object to serving under 'offensive' officers. Attitudes on both sides were harder. The Government and the Admiralty were determined to make no further concessions; the sailors blockaded merchant ships using the port of London, except for those containing perishable goods. Like the Spithead mutineers, the sailors at the Nore continued to protest their loyalty to King and country: on the King's birthday they fired a gun salute. In spite of this, and although no direct connections with Jacobins or radical working men's Corresponding Societies were ever proved, there were far more political undertones. The ringleader,

Richard Parker, styled himself 'president'; in some of their manifestoes the men referred to themselves as 'the victims of tyranny' and saluted the dawn of the 'Age of Reason'. But these wider, political aims were never made fully manifest, and the methods and the ends remained muddled and confused. Certainly the majority of the sailors did not support such aims, and the mutinous ships gradually sailed away to surrender. Twenty-nine of the ringleaders were executed; nine were flogged; and twenty-nine imprisoned. Parker himself, an educated man, who had previously served as a midshipman but had been court-martialled for disobedience, died bravely, but a despondent man.

Other mutinies occurred during the next few years at the Cape, in the West Indies, and at Cadiz, but these were crushed on the spot.

In addition to the increase in pay, there were some other improvements in the Royal Navy during the eighteenth century. The weekly rations at the beginning of the century were very little different from what they had been in earlier times. In 1729 they were:

Bread	1 lb a day
Beer	1 gallon a day
Beef	2 lb on Tuesday and Saturday
Pork	1 lb on Sunday and Thursday
Pease	$\frac{1}{2}$ pint on Sunday, Wednesday, Thursday, Friday
Oatmeal	1 pint on Monday, Wednesday and Friday
Butter	2 oz on Monday, Wednesday and Saturday
Cheese	4 oz on Monday, Wednesday and Friday

(Quoted in Edgar K. Thompson: 'Sea Fare of Seafarers', in *The Mariner's Mirror*, volume 54, Cambridge University Press, 1968)

On longer cruises particularly, the beer became so flat and sour that it became a common practice to replace it with a pint of wine a day or half a pint of rum. The issue of rum was a mixed blessing, because this stronger drink led to much drunkenness, which often resulted in the offender being flogged. In 1740 Admiral Vernon ordered that the rum should be diluted. This drink was called 'grog', after the material, grogram, from which the Admiral's cloak was made. Even then the drink was still so strong that it caused drunkenness, and the amount of water was progressively increased. Cocoa and tea were introduced towards the end of the century. Portable soup—in the form of dried cubes—and sauerkraut, or pickled cabbage, were both introduced during the century, but neither were at first very popular with sailors. After the Spithead and Nore mutinies more ships started to call at overseas ports to stock up with fresh meat and vegetables.

The biggest reform was the issue of a daily ration of lemon juice in 1795. More than forty years before that, Dr James Lind, a naval surgeon, had proved conclusively by controlled experiments that lemons or oranges could cure the dreaded disease of scurvy, from which so many seamen had died on longer voyages. (Dr Lind established the cure, but it was not until the twentieth century that the cause was discovered: a lack of Vitamin C, which is contained in lemons, oranges and fresh vegetables.)

On the 20th May, 1747, I took twelve patients in the scurvy on board the *Salisbury* at sea. Their cases were as similar as I could have them. . . . Two of these were ordered each a quart of cyder a day. Two others took . . . elixir vitriol three times a day. . . . Two others took two spoonfuls of vinegar three times a day. . . . Two of the worst patients . . . were put under a course of sea water. Two others had each two oranges and one lemon given them every day. . . . The two remaining patients took . . . three times a day of an electuary[5] recommended by an hospital surgeon. . . .

The consequence was that the most sudden and visible good effects were perceived from the use of the oranges and lemons; one of those who had taken them being at the end of six days fit for duty. . . . The other was the best recovered of any in his condition. . . .

(Dr James Lind: *A Treatise of the Scurvy*, Edinburgh, 1753)

A number of Tudor seamen, like Sir Richard Hawkins, had also recommended the use of 'sowre Oranges and Lemmons' as the best cure for scurvy, but he also proposed other remedies, including dancing, watered wine or beer, and sprinkling the ship with vinegar. Dr Lind had proved conclusively that oranges and lemons were a certain cure, but it took the Admiralty another forty years to introduce it, largely because of the extra expense. Scurvy continued to plague the Merchant Navy for many more years: in 1854 masters were compelled to serve crews with lemon or lime juice—a somewhat less efficacious remedy—after they had been on salt meat for ten days.

[5] A medicine mixed with honey or syrup.

3

During the eighteenth century Britain climbed towards the peak of her maritime power. The unprecedented expansion in trade, particularly during the second half of the century as Britain became the first nation to industrialize, brought about a great increase in the size of the merchant fleet. From an estimated 323 000 tons at the beginning of the century, it had grown to 1 855 000 tons by the end. By present-day standards the ships were all very small. The largest, of 1 200 tons or so, were employed in the China trade, but the vast majority were under 200 tons. The larger merchant vessels of 200 or 300 tons or more were practically all three-masted and most of them had two or three decks.

To protect merchant ships in time of war, and to defend the country from invasion, a bigger Navy was needed. In 1793 there were 411 ships—brigs of 380 tons or so, frigates of 900 tons, and first-rate ships of over 2 000 tons.[6] By 1814, when the Royal Navy had emerged triumphant from a life or death struggle with Napoleonic France, the total number of ships had passed the thousand mark.

4

1704	Pauper boys over ten forced to become apprentices in Merchant Navy
1731	First Admiralty regulations relating to discipline
1740	Grog introduced by Admiral Vernon
1756	Marine Society formed by Jonas Hanway
1775	Liverpool seamen's riot
1795	Quota Acts
1795	Daily issue of lemon juice introduced in Navy

[6] Warships were rated from one to six according to the number of guns. Though there were some variations, the first-rate had 100–110 guns; second-rate, 90–100; third-rate, 80–84; fourth-rate, 60–74; fifth-rate, 32–40; and the sixth-rate, any number, usually 24. The complements varied from 800–875 for a first-rate, to 150 for a sixth-rate.

1797   Spithead and Nore mutinies
1797   Wages of able seamen increased to 29*s.* 6*d.* a month and those
        of ordinary seamen to 23*s.* 6*d.*

For Further Reading
J. R. Hutchinson, *The Press-Gang Afloat and Ashore*, London, 1913

Part Four

Nelson's Navy

1

There was always another side to life in the Royal Navy. Rough and tough though the sailors were, they had their own rigid standards of value, and would give unlimited respect and loyalty to a good officer. An officer could gain this respect, or sometimes even veneration, by his courage, his fairness, his success in battle or in capturing prizes. During the Spithead mutiny unpopular officers were expelled from their ships; over a hundred in all, including Admiral Gardner. Only six out of twenty-one officers were allowed to remain aboard the *Duke*. But those officers whom the men admired continued to remain popular, mutiny or no mutiny. Captain Talbot, of the frigate *Eurydice*, who had gone ashore voluntarily, was summoned back to his ship by his crew.

> Captain Talbot . . . we now join our earnest wishes and desires that you will once more join the flock of which you are the tender shepherd. We wish by this to show you, Sir, that we are men that loves the present cause as men ought to, yet we are not eleveated that degree to neglect our duty to our country or our obedience to you, and . . . the command of the ship belongs to you, sir, which command we, the ship's company, resign with all due honour, respect and submission hopeing you will always continue to do as you have heretofore done, to hear a man's cause as well as an officer's.
>
> (Quoted in Manwaring and Dobrée, op. cit.)

In fact, it had been one of the sailors' chief grievances for many years that they could not continue to serve under an officer they liked and follow him from ship to ship. One officer who commanded this respect above all others was Nelson. When it became known in June

1800 that he was about to leave the *Foudroyant* his barge crew wrote to him:

> My Lord,
> It is with extreme grief that we find you are about to leave us. We have been along with you (although not in the same Ship) in every Engagement your Lordship has been in, both by Sea and Land; and most humbly beg of your Lordship to permit us to go to England, as your Boat's crew, in any Ship or Vessel, or in any way that may seem most pleasing to your Lordship. . . .
>
> (Quoted in Moorhouse, op. cit.)

The gulf between even the lowest-ranking officer and sailor was very wide, so that there could be no real communication between them. But the best officers, like Nelson, all had a sincere, even if unspoken, sympathy for their men.

> I believe the world is convinced that no conquests of importance can be made without us; and yet, as soon as we have accomplished the service we are ordered on, we are neglected. If Parliament does not grant something to this Fleet, our Jacks will grumble; for here there is no prize-money to soften their hardships; all we get is honour and salt beef. My poor fellows have not had a morsel of fresh meat or vegetables for near nineteen weeks; and in that time I have only had my foot twice on shore at Cadiz. No Fleet, I am certain, ever served their country with greater zeal than this has done, from the Admiral to the lowest sailor.
>
> (Nelson to his wife, 11th September 1793, in Sir Nicholas Harris Nicolas, editor: *The Dispatches and Letters of Vice Admiral Lord Viscount Nelson*, Vol. 1 London, 1844)

Who were these men who fought with Nelson against the French? Because the press-gang often took foreign seamen out of merchant ships, not all of them were British. As Christopher Lloyd, one of the most eminent naval historians, has shown by his examination of the 1805 muster-book of Nelson's *Victory*, 48 of the 628 men aboard had foreign birth-places. Twenty-three had been born in America, and others in Holland, Sweden, Denmark, Prussia, Africa, Switzerland—even one in France! About half were pressed men (319 in all), which was probably the average proportion at that time; later in the war it may have risen to three-quarters, though there is no real certainty about these figures. And, very surprisingly, there were often a few women aboard these warships, even when they were at sea.

Whenever a ship reached harbour wives and prostitutes came aboard in hordes.

> The whole of the shocking, disgraceful transactions of the lower deck it is impossible to describe:—the dirt, filth, and stench; the disgusting conversation; the indecent, beastly conduct and horrible scenes; the blasphemy and swearing; the riots, quarrels, and fightings, which often take place, where hundreds of men and women are huddled together in one room as it were. . . .
>
> (Anon: *Statement of Certain Immoral Practices prevailing in His Majesty's Navy,* London, 1822, 2nd. ed.)

Although many officers were shocked by these drunken orgies, the only alternative was to grant shore leave, which very few captains were willing to do. When the ship put out to sea again it was not unknown for one or two of the more enterprising women to hide themselves away. Some captains allowed a few wives to accompany sailors on non-operational cruises, though they were banned on active service. Even then, however, there were usually one or two women aboard, as there were in some of Nelson's warships during his major battles with the Spanish and the French. The women were employed in caring for the wounded and in carrying the powder. A number of them were wounded, and one woman had a baby during the battle of the Nile.

John Nicol served aboard the *Goliath* both in the battle of St Vincent on 14th February 1797 and in the battle of the Nile (or Aboukir Bay) on 1st August 1798. His description of Nelson's great victories is so full of enthralling detail, and illustrates the views of one representative member of the lower deck so well, that it is worth quoting at some length.

> While we lay at Lisbon we got private intelligence overland that the Spanish fleet was at sea. We with all dispatch set sail in pursuit of them. We were so fortunate as to come in sight of them by break of day, on the 14th of February, off Cape St Vincent. They consisted of twenty-five sail, mostly three-deckers. We were only eighteen; but we were English. . . . Soon as we came in sight, a bustle commenced, not to be conceived or described. To do it justice, while every man was as busy as he could be, the greatest order prevailed. A serious cast was to be perceived on every face; but not a shade of doubt or fear. We rejoiced in a general action; not that we loved fighting; but we all wished to be free to return to our homes, and follow our own pursuits. We knew there was no other way of obtaining this than by defeating the enemy. . . .

When everything was cleared, the ports open, the matches lighted, the guns run out, then we gave them three such cheers as are only to be heard in a British man-of-war. . . . I was stationed in the after magazine, serving powder from the screen, and could see nothing; but I could feel every shot that struck the Goliah, and the cries and groans of the wounded were most distressing, as there was only the thickness of the blankets of the screen between me and them. . . . Those who were carrying run like wild creatures, and scarce opened their lips. The Goliah was sore beset; for some time she had two three-deckers upon her. The men stood to their guns as cool as if they had been exercising. The Admiral ordered the Britannia to our assistance. Iron-sides, with her forty-twos, soon made them sheer off. . . .[1]

At length the roar of the guns cease, and I came on deck to see the effects of a great sea engagement; but such a scene of blood and desolation I want words to express. . . . We had destroyed a great number, and secured four three-deckers. . . . The fleet was in such a shattered situation, we lay twenty-four hours in sight of them, repairing our rigging. . . . Captain Sir C. H. Knowles [their captain] was tried for not lending assistance, when he needed it himself. The court-martial honourably acquitted him. Collis, our first lieutenant, told us not to cheer when he came on board; but we loved our captain too well to be restrained. . . . We manned the yards, and gave three hearty cheers. Not a man on board but would have bled for Sir C. H. Knowles. . . .

We got intelligence that the French fleet were up the Straights. We then made sail for Egypt. . . . We fell in with a French brig, who had just left the fleet. Admiral Nelson took her in tow, and she conducted us to where they lay at anchor in Aboukir Bay.

My station was in the powder magazine with the gunner. As we entered the bay, we stripped to our trowsers, opened our ports, cleared, and every ship we passed we gave them a broad-side and three cheers. Any information we got was from the boys and women who carried the powder. . . . When the French Admiral's ship blew up, the Goliah got such a shake, we thought the after-part of her had blown up until the boys told us what it was. They brought us every now and then the cheering news of another French ship having struck, and we answered the cheers on deck with heart-felt joy. In the heat of the action, a shot came right into the magazine, but did no harm, as the carpenters plugged it up, and stopped the water that was rushing in. . . . There were some of the women wounded, and one woman belonging to Leith died of her wounds. . . . One woman bore a son in the heat of the action; she belonged to the Edinburgh. When we ceased firing, I went on deck to view the state

[1] The Britannia is a first-rate, carrying 110 guns. She was the only ship that carried 42 pounders on her lower deck, and 32 on her middle deck. She was the strongest built ship in the navy; the sailors upon this account called her 'Iron-sides'. [Footnote in the original.]

of the fleets, and an awful sight it was. The whole bay was covered with dead bodies, mangled, wounded, and scorched, not a bit of clothes on them except their trowsers. . . .

The only incidents I heard of are two. One lad who was stationed by a salt-box, on which he sat to give out cartridges . . . when asked for a cartridge, he gave none, yet he sat upright; his eyes were open. One of the men gave him a push; he fell all his length on the deck. There was not a blemish on his body, yet he was quite dead, and was thrown overboard. The other, a lad who had the match in his hand to fire his gun. In the act of applying it a shot took off his arm; it hung by a small piece of skin. The match fell to the deck. He looked to his arm, and seeing what had happened, seized the match in his left hand, and fired off the gun before he went to the cock-pit[2] to have it dressed. They were in our mess, or I might never have heard of it. Two of the mess were killed, and I knew not of it until the day after. Thus terminated the glorious first of August, the busiest night of my life.

(John Nicol, op. cit.)

[2] The after part of the lowest deck, used by the surgeons during a battle.

Orme: Nelson coming on deck during the Battle of the Nile.
National Maritime Museum

Many gunners were remote from the battle, working half-naked in the stifling heat of the gun-decks, where shot was put in furnaces until it was white-hot, and then taken in long-handled shot-carriers to the guns, where it was discharged in an attempt to set enemy ships on fire. The gun-crews tied a handkerchief around their ears to muffle the noise of the explosions: many of them were deaf for weeks after a battle. The gunners, marines and boarding parties (on the upper decks) armed with cutlasses and cudgels, saw more of the action, in spite of the billowing clouds of smoke from explosions and ships which had been set on fire. It was there, 'amid the bustle' of the battle, Nicol says rather regretfully, that he would rather have been, where time seemed to fly 'on eagle's wings'. But the warships depended on the efficiency and accuracy of these hidden men—the 15-man crews of each 32-pounder, nine feet long, which could hurl a shot, six inches in diameter, a distance of $1\frac{1}{2}$ miles, and which fired at close range could penetrate three feet of oak. The carronade, a shorter gun, mounted on the upper deck, which weighed only half of the 32-pounder's three tons, could blast a 68lb shot through the stoutest timbers at short range. It was with the carronade that Nelson's *Victory* opened fire at Trafalgar, hurling it through the stern of the *Bucentaure*, where it did great damage. In spite of the destructive power of these weapons, fired at close range, casualties were small: at Trafalgar only 449 were killed and 1 241 wounded out of the 18 725 men engaged. Disease and accidents were the great killers in the Navy: they accounted for more than 80 per cent of the 100 000 or more seamen who were killed during the wars against Revolutionary France and Napoleon from 1793 to 1815.

Nelson, however, in full dress, with his many decorations glittering on the left breast of his coat, presented an easy target. A midshipman aboard the *Victory* wrote to his parents after the engagement:

> I have just time and opportunity to tell you that we had a desperate engagement with the enemy, and, thank God, I have so far escaped unhurt. . . .
>
> I am sorry—very sorry—to tell you that amongst the slain is Lord Nelson, his secretary, Mr. Scott, and Mr. Whipple, Captain Hardy's clerk, whom you know. . . .
>
> Admiral Nelson was shot early in the action by a musket ball from the enemy's top, which struck him a little below the shoulder, touched the rib and lodged near his heart. He lived about $2\frac{1}{2}$ hours after; then died without a groan. . . .
>
> *(An Account of Trafalgar by Midshipman Roberts,*
> quoted in Moorhouse, op. cit.)

Thus died England's greatest naval hero, mourned by the nation, his brother officers, and the men who had served under him. His body was brought back to England, and lay in state at Greenwich for three days before it was taken up river in a barge procession for burial in St Paul's Cathedral. An hour before the lying-in-state ended on 7th January 1806, a brig, *Elizabeth and Mary*, came sailing up the river.

> She had on board a chosen band of seamen and marines from the brave crew of the *Victory*, destined to form a part of the funeral procession of their noble commander. . . . They consisted of 46 seamen and 14 marines, and most of them bore the honourable scars they received on the day that deprived them of their chief. . . . They were met by Lord Hood, who told the gallant tars that they should be gratified with a sight of the body of their heroic leader lying in state, though, he added, he was sure it would be to them no pleasant spectacle.

> (Josuah White: *Supplement to the Life of the Late Horatio Lord Viscount Nelson*, London, 1806.)

Nelson lying in state in the Painted Chamber at Greenwich Hospital.
National Maritime Museum

2

In the year that Nelson was buried, sailors were given a pay increase. The able seaman got 4*s*. more, bringing his wages up to 33*s*. 6*d*. a month, and the ordinary seaman got 2*s*. more, increasing his pay to 25*s*. 6*d*. It wasn't much of a pay rise—the ordinary seamen still received less than a soldier—but it was a much greater reward for the victory of Trafalgar than the sailors who defeated the Spanish Armada, more than two hundred years earlier, had ever got. They had been left to die in the streets.

The wars against France also brought a slightly greater chance of promotion to officer rank. Professor Michael Lewis has estimated that a sailor's chances of getting a commission were one in 2 500, but very few of those promoted ever attained a higher rank than that of lieutenant. After the war, when the Navy was drastically reduced in size, and promotion was blocked even for most officers, the chances were practically nil.

3

Horatio Nelson did more than any other man to save Britain from invasion by Napoleon, through his great victories at sea. He became a legend in his own lifetime for his brilliant tactics, his great personal courage, and his concern for those who served under him. Born in 1758, the son of a Norfolk clergyman, he joined the Navy in 1770. In 1794, while taking part in the land fighting during the invasion of Corsica, he lost the sight of his right eye. Three years later he made a major contribution to the victory off Cape St Vincent, when 15 British ships defeated 27 Spanish ships. After his ship, the *Captain*, had been badly damaged, Commodore Nelson ordered it to be brought close to a Spanish warship, and was one of the first men to go aboard. When the ship had been captured he used it to board another Spanish warship, thus breaking the enemy's line. For his part in this battle he was made a K.B. In the same year he lost his right arm in an unsuccessful expedition against the Spanish in the Canary Islands.

In the following year, 1798, at the battle of the Nile, his ships overwhelmingly defeated a French fleet in Aboukir Bay. Some of Nelson's ships attacked from the sea, while others sailed in behind the French, running the risk of grounding on the shore. Only two of the thirteen French warships escaped. For this great victory he was created Baron Nelson of the Nile. In 1801, as second-in-command to Sir Hyde Parker, Nelson's twelve ships sailed into the heavily de-fended port of Copenhagen to attack the Danish fleet. It was during this action that Nelson put his telescope to his sightless eye, when his commander ran up flags signalling him to break off the action. Nelson went on, and destroyed most of the Danish fleet.

The victory for which he will always be remembered came in 1805 at the battle of Trafalgar. Nelson's twenty-seven ships defeated a combined fleet of thirty-three French and Spanish warships. The enemy lost twenty vessels. Nelson was shot by a sniper, and died in the hour of his greatest triumph, but his victory saved the country and Napoleon had to call off his plans to invade Britain.

4

1797   Battle of St Vincent
1798   Battle of the Nile
1801   Battle of Copenhagen
1805   Battle of Trafalgar
1806   Nelson buried in St Paul's
1806   Able seamen's pay increased to 33*s.* 6*d.* a month and ordinary
          seaman's to 25*s.* 6*d.*

For Further Reading
Edward Fraser, *The Sailors whom Nelson Led: their doings described by themselves*, Methuen, 1913
David Howarth: *Trafalgar, the Nelson Touch*, Collins, 1969
Michael Lewis: *A Social History of the Navy, 1793–1815*, Allen and Unwin, 1960

Part Five

Britannia Rules the Waves

1

Britain emerged victorious from the Napoleonic wars as the major maritime Power, a position that she was to retain against all challengers for more than a century. During the nineteenth century the Royal Navy—the strongest in the world—was to become completely distinct from the merchant service for the first time, with different crews, different ships and different conditions of service. Immediately after the end of hostilities with France, the number of ships and men in the Royal Navy was drastically reduced. The Admiralty's problem was no longer how to impress men but how to get rid of most of those it had as quickly as possible to save money. By 1817 the total number of men had been reduced from over 130 000 to just over 20 000.

In the 1820s life and work for those who remained aboard H.M. ships was more or less the same as it had been before the wars, but with an even greater emphasis on cleanliness and un-questioning—and immediate—obedience to orders, which was imposed by a liberal use of the cat-o'-nine tails. Charles McPherson, who joined the Navy as a young lad in the 1820s, gives a graphic picture of his first morning aboard a warship.

I was awakened, after a comfortable night's sleep, by the sound of the boatswain's pipe turning the hands up to wash decks. I jumped out of my hammock, and forgetting in the dark that my companion slept so close to me, I fell plump on top of him. . . . On reaching deck, I got a holy-stone[1] placed in my hand, and was told to lend a hand in scrubbing the boards. It was a cold January morning, a strong sharp east wind was blowing at the

[1] Holy-stones are smooth sand stones, and are rubbed on the deck after it is wet and sanded, which makes the deck appear, when dry, of a beautiful white. [Footnote in the original.]

time; we were obliged to go on our knees on the wet decks, and my fingers got so benumbed that they could scarcely hold the stone. . . . I was a little better pleased, however, when they piped to breakfast; and, going down to the mess, I found a large basin of cocoa ready for me, and plenty of biscuit. . . . We had salt beef and pudding this day to dinner, which I liked better than the raw pork.

(A British Seaman [Charles McPherson]: *Life on Board a Man-of-War*, Glasgow, 1829)

In the years of comparative peace which succeeded one of Britain's longest wars sweeping and scrubbing became the order of the day.

A Frigate's Lower Deck may be kept perfectly clean thus:—
Dry-holystone it once a day. After every meal, give every spot of dirt, a touch of the stone again; and, before and after every meal, sweep the Berths clean out, and sweep clean fore and aft. Once a week, get every chest and other obstruction off the deck, dry-holystone with more than ordinary care, and sweep all clean with scrupulous attention. Wet-holystone only after any particularly dirty extra work, such as provisioning or cleaning the holds. . . .

(Lieut. Alex Dingwall Fordyce R.N.: *Outlines of Naval Routine*, London, 1837)

The same officer placed a similar emphasis on cleanliness and smartness in his suggested sea routine for a typical day:

3.30	Get ready for washing decks
4.00	Scrub upper deck and all windsails, cots, boat's sails, etc. requiring it
Day-light	Take off look-out men on deck, and place them at masthead
6.00	Make and reset sail
6.45	Lash up hammocks
7.00	Muster and stow ditto
7.10	Clean arms
7.25	Watch flemish[2] ropes and spread awning
7.25	Watch below clean Lower Deck
8.00	Breakfast
8.30	Clean in working clothes
9.00	Stow bags and sweep Decks
9.30	Divisions
10.00	Work or Exercise of Arms or Guns by Watch
11.30	Clear Decks and up Spirits

[2] To coil

12.00	Dinner
1.00	Down windsails, cots etc.
1.15	Sweep up decks
1.30	Work or Exercise of Arms or Guns by Watch
2.00	Pump water and serve out
4.10	Clear decks and furl awning
5.00	Supper
5.30	Quarters—keys returned
	General exercise of Guns or Sails
5.50	Ropes down in round Coils
Dusk	Place Look-outs on Deck, and call
	Mast-head men down
8.00	Down Hammocks
8.10	Ship's Company Fire and Lights out
9.00	Steerage lights out
10.00	Gun-room lights out

(Ibid.)

Throughout the centuries the daily routine changed just as slowly as the ships themselves. These had slowly evolved from the old 'round ships' of Tudor times, with their high castles fore and aft, into longer, sleeker, larger warships, like the *Victory*, with its slightly raised stern and tall sides. During the first quarter of the nineteenth century the ships were still built of wood and powered by sails, while the guns they carried were only a little more powerful than those which had been used to defeat the Spanish Armada. The last great battle under sail took place in 1827, when a squadron of British, Russian and French ships defeated the combined fleets of Turkey and Egypt during the Greek War of Independence.

In the first half of the century increasing co-operation between Governments made it possible for the Royal Navy to act as the guardian of the world's oceans, arresting slave-ships and detaining pirates. Denmark abolished the slave trade in 1792, Britain and the United States in 1807, followed by many other countries from 1814 onwards. Britain concluded treaties with a large number of states, giving her the right to search suspected ships for slaves. The British, who from the seventeenth century had been one of the major slave-trading nations, now became the world's policemen: the vast profits from that trade were replaced by small amounts of prize-money, paid from 1815 to 1854 to crews of ships who rescued slaves. The Admiralty issued strict instructions how both slaves and slave-traders should be treated.

You will take special care to ensure propriety of language and de-
meanour on the part of Officers, seamen and marines, towards all persons
with whom they may come into contact in the service of suppressing the
Slave Trade; and they must be reminded that any breach of discipline, or
any exhibition of intemperance, will be visited with severe punishment. . . .

If Slaves should be on board, every effort is to be made to alleviate their
sufferings and improve their condition, by a careful attention to cleanliness and ventilation, by separating the sickly from those who are in good
health, by encouraging the Slaves to feel confidence in Her Majesty's
officers and men, and promoting among them cheerfulness and exercise.

(Instructions for the guidance of Her Majesty's Naval Officers employed
in the suppression of the Slave Trade, London, 1844)

In the early years of the nineteenth century Barbary pirates
continued to plague merchant ships in the Mediterranean. Tom
Morfiet was one of the few sailors who were lucky enough to survive
the ordeal of walking the plank.

His father had been a merchant in the Isle of Guernsey, [and] at one
time had several vessels in the Levant trade, but, through crosses in the
world, was obliged to take the only vessel left him, a brig of 150 tons, and
go as a master on a voyage to Smyrna, to try and retrieve his fortune. He
took along with him, to assist him in working the vessel, three sons,
between the ages of 18 and 25, and had proceeded on his voyage as far as
the island of Cerigo, when the brig was boarded by a Turkish pirate, and
the father and three sons were obliged to *walk the plank* i.e. after having
their hands tied behind their backs, and their eyes blindfolded, they were
made to mount a plank projecting from the vessel's side and walk
overboard. When the news of this reached Guernsey, his mother, whose
mind had been previously unhinged by the sudden reverse of fortune,
went completely deranged, and died in a mad-house. Poor Tom, then
very young, was the only survivor. . . .

(Charles McPherson, op. cit.)

The activities of the Barbary pirates were greatly curtailed after the
French occupied their main base of Algiers in 1830, and the Royal
Navy started stronger patrols in the Mediterranean.

Privateers continued to operate, too, until they were abolished by
most countries under the terms of the Treaty of Paris in 1856.
Previously some enterprising British seamen had continued to get
letters of marque from foreign Powers, as sixteen British seamen did
in 1818 during the revolt of the South American colonies against
Spanish rule, when they captured an armed Spanish merchant ship
and had it recognized as a prize.

British sailors boarding an Algerian pirate ship.
National Maritime Museum

The English tars soon found themselves in the possession of what appeared to them inexhaustible riches. They would not have been true British seamen, however, had they hoarded up their wealth.... They gave balls, grand theatrical parties, and all sorts of sumptuous entertainment.... In a few years ... some of them ... again found themselves before the mast in Lord Cochrane's fleet; while others more provident, established themselves as respectable and substantial citizens. Mackay became one of the most considerable of the merchants and shipowners in Valparaiso....

(Anon: *The Wonderful Adventures of Sixteen British Seamen*,
Glasgow, n.d.)

It was after the first quarter of the nineteenth century that the modern Navy was created. In 1826 a new rating of stoker was introduced. Steam was on its way. By 1828 the first four ships, equipped with both sails and paddle-wheels driven by a steam-engine, had been commissioned. On the eve of the Crimean War there were 74 steam-vessels out of a total of 201 ships. The Admiralty were not very enthusiastic about the first steam-vessels: paddle-wheels could easily be shot away by the enemy, and they also reduced the arc of fire. But the screw propeller had proved its worth by the 1850s, and the days of sail were then numbered. Later in the century the screw was replaced by the much more powerful steam turbine, invented by Sir Charles Parsons, in which jets of steam are directed on to the blades of a rotating shaft. It was first tested in 1897 in the *Turbinia,* a small 100-foot craft which reached a speed of 34 knots. The steam turbine was soon afterwards adopted by both the Navy and the merchant service.

By then the 'wooden walls' which had protected Britain throughout the centuries had also been replaced by iron ships. In January 1861 the *Warrior* was launched: it was the first real ironclad with both an iron hull and armour plating to protect the guns on the main deck.

> Day by day this noble frigate continues to advance rapidly towards completion, and there seems little doubt but that in the course of six weeks or so more she will be in a condition to go round under steam to Portsmouth, where she is to be rigged and masted and got ready for sea with all despatch. But with a new vessel of such an entirely experimental character as this armour ship, innumerable details have to be considered. . . . The labour of putting on the enormous armour-plates, which are all dovetailed into each other, is one which must necessarily be slowly completed. With three engines and her street of boilers in her vast hold, it is confidently anticipated that she will attain a speed hitherto unknown in the Navy. . . . The *Warrior* will have two funnels, each 8 feet in diameter and 25 feet above the deck. . . . Taken altogether, the machinery required for propulsion will weigh 890 tons—a great weight, certainly, though not so much when one remembers that the power exerted by it will be little short of 6 000 horses. . . .
>
> (*The Times*, March 30, 1861)

There were improvements in ordnance too, with the introduction of heavier, breech-loading guns, with rifled bores, which could hurl a heavy shell for many miles. The pace of technological change was so rapid that by the time of the naval manoeuvres of 1899 warships already had a recognizably modern air.

> We departed, through sundry massive water-tight doors . . . into a spacious compartment extending right across the ship, the after submerged torpedo room. . . .
>
> Everything here, far below the water-line, was, if possible, brighter and cleaner than anything I had yet seen on board—it glittered under the electric lamps like a first-class jeweller's shop window.

And so we fared onward through dynamo room, hydraulic room, air-compressing room, taking occasional peeps at gauges revealing pressures up to 1 300lb or 1 400lb to the square inch. . . .

Everywhere we came upon quiet, studious-looking men clad in the well-known duck[3] jumper and trousers of working men-of-war's men. . . . Into a large, well-appointed workshop, fitted with all the machinery for repairs or replacements . . . by devious ways into the foundations of the barbettes,[4] where lay the forces that at a finger's touch . . . manipulated the two 46-ton guns like toys. . . .

(Frank T. Bullen: *The Way they have in the Navy, being a day-to-day record of a cruise in H.M. Battleship 'Mars' during the Naval Manoeuvres of 1899*, London, 1899)

At the beginning of the present century there was an even more important development, which was to revolutionize the whole of naval warfare—the introduction of submarines.

The first five British submarines are almost identically the same as the six Holland boats ordered by the U.S. Congress on June 7, 1900.

They are cigar-shaped vessels, 63 feet 4 inches long; beam 11 feet 9 inches; and displacement submerged, 120 tons. The plating and frames are of steel and of sufficient size and thickness to withstand the pressure of depths not exceeding 100 feet.

The first British submarine was launched on November 2, 1901, at Barrow without any ceremony, although representatives of the Admiralty were present. . . . .

Before launching 'No. 1' was by means of a floating dock placed on the gridiron.[5] A crew of six men were put on board, and she was then hermetically sealed for three hours, air being supplied by compressed air cylinders. The trial was quite successful, and the men suffered no inconvenience. . . . .

The first submersion trials of 'No. 1' were carried out on February 5, 1902.

(Herbert C. Fyfe: *Submarine Warfare, Past, Present and Future*, London, 1902)

Four years later, in 1906, Britain launched the turbine-driven *Dreadnought*, the first of a new class of battleships, which could outsail and outgun any other battleship afloat. Other nations built battleships of a similar design, and super-Dreadnoughts with a higher

[3] Strong linen or cotton.
[4] Gun platform.
[5] A frame of parallel beams supporting a ship in dock.

The second British submarine lying alongside a gunboat in 1902.
Imperial War Museum

speed of 25 knots were launched. But by 1914 Britain was still in the lead, with half as many dreadnoughts again as her nearest rival—Germany.

2

During the second half of the nineteenth century there was an immense improvement in conditions in the Royal Navy. Impressment was abandoned and long-term engagements instituted in its place; food was improved; punishments were mitigated; pay was increased, and pensions for long-serving sailors were introduced. The pleas made by the mutinous sailors in Drake's expeditions of 1587 that they should be treated like men, not beasts, were finally answered. The long delay in doing so cannot be attributed entirely to callous indifference to the men's sufferings; it was occasioned just as much by the generally slow pace of change in maritime affairs during the three preceding centuries. The improvements that were made in Victorian times were a direct result of the revolution brought about by technology, which created a demand for a different kind of educated man with various specialized skills; the nation's increasing wealth and power which made it possible to pay for a standing navy; and the slowly changing attitudes in society itself towards the men of the lower deck. The gulf between officer and men remained wide, but among the Victorian public at least there was an increasing admiration for 'jolly Jack Tar', and an increasing appreciation of his worth.

Impressment was not officially abolished, but there was very little need of it in the post-Napoleonic period, when massive unemployment induced enough men to volunteer for service in the greatly reduced number of warships. During the Crimean War it proved just about possible to man the fleets without bringing back the press-gang, largely because the war was not primarily a naval one. A year before the war broke out the first of the major reforms had been introduced. In 1853 men could make a career in the Royal Navy by signing on for ten years under the continuous service system.

The new long-term engagements, with their slightly higher rates of pay, did not satisfy all sailors. Four seamen were called to give evidence to the Royal Commission on Manning the Navy, which reported in 1859. Three of them had to be encouraged to express their complaints; but John Donelly, an Irish seaman rigger, who had served his time in the merchant service before he joined the Navy, was quite undeterred by the presence of admirals on the Commission.

Is there anything with regard to the treatment of the seamen on board a man-of-war that you think is likely to lead to the unpopularity of the Navy in the minds of English sailors everywhere?—The wages are rather small for instance, and the consequence is, that there is a boy of the first-rate rated an ordinary seamen, and he is on the new scale for continuous service; shortly after he is rated an able seaman, and that boy receives the same pay, in fact more than I do. . . . I receive £2 a month, and he receives £2 9s. 4d. . . . What prevents your going upon the new scale?—The only objection that I have ever known about it is that many men do not fancy it. Perhaps I have got into a ship where the discipline is very strict and the consequence is I may think I have only about eighteen months or two years to run, and the ship will be paid off. . . . Perhaps you will state two or three leading reasons why you think the merchant service would be more pleasant to you than the navy?—It is pleasanter in some respects, but not in others. In the navy you are clean and comfortable; in the merchant service you are dirty, and there are many things of that kind; you cannot have your grub properly, but you have more of it, you can go and cut off a joint of meat....

(Reports of the Commissioners appointed to inquire
into the best means of Manning the Navy,
Parliamentary Papers, Vol. 6, 1859.)

The complaints about food—one of the long-standing grievances of sailors—were reiterated by another witness, Joseph Burney, a seaman rigger from Plymouth Dockyard.

I think that a man could do with half a pound of bread more; the bread is very short; the one pound of bread; it is not sufficient for a man, particularly a young man ... and the next thing is your vegetables, you are allowed half a pound, what is that? It is only pumpkins, what you get in foreign places....

(Ibid.)

The Royal Commission took some notice of the seamen's complaints and recommended an increase in the rations, which was introduced in 1867.

Daily	Biscuit	$1\frac{1}{4}$ lb
	or	
	Soft Bread	$1\frac{1}{2}$ lb
	Spirit	$\frac{1}{8}$ pint
	Sugar	2 oz
	Chocolate	1 oz
	Tea	$\frac{1}{4}$ oz
Weekly	Oatmeal	3 oz
	Mustard	$\frac{1}{2}$ oz
	Pepper	$\frac{1}{4}$ oz
	Vinegar	$\frac{1}{4}$ pint
Daily, when	Fresh meat	1 lb
procurable	Vegetables	$\frac{1}{2}$ lb

(*Scale of Victualling in Her Majesty's Navy,*
Admiralty, 1st August, 1867)

On days when fresh meat and vegetables could not be obtained the men were given salt meat, or tinned meat, which had first been tried out in the Navy in 1813. On alternate days they received 1 lb of salt pork and $\frac{3}{4}$ lb of split peas which was made into soup; 1 lb of salt beef and 9 oz of flour, $\frac{3}{4}$ oz of suet and $1\frac{1}{2}$ oz of currants or raisins for making a suet pudding; or $\frac{3}{4}$ lb of preserved beef with preserved potatoes or rice.

These rations provided a reasonable dinner by the standards of those times, but all the sailor got for breakfast was a bowl of cocoa and ship's biscuit, and for supper a dish of tea and biscuit again. The quality of the food also left much to be desired, as one man complained in 1877.

> The salt beef and pork varies in quality according to the time it has been in salt, which, in these days of fast steamers, is unnecessarily long. The beef is very often mistaken by the uninitiated for a piece of wood, and it is sometimes hard to convince visitors on board ship to the contrary.
>
> Preserved Irish beef . . . is very much overcooked in the preserving, as it takes the form of a conglomeration of strings when warmed for eating, so much so, that it has earned for itself the cognomen of 'Clews[6] and lashings'.
>
> (Anon: *The Seamen of the Royal Navy, their advantages and disadvantages as viewed from the Lower Deck*, London, 1877)

As the century progressed canteens became increasingly common on naval ships. There, sailors could supplement their diet with other kinds of food—butter, jam and cake, for example—but they had to buy these extras out of their wages. At the beginning of the present century a more varied scale of rations was introduced.

Daily	$1\frac{1}{4}$ lb biscuit or soft bread
	2 oz Jam
	$\frac{1}{8}$ pint of spirit
	$\frac{1}{2}$ oz coffee
	3 oz sugar
	4 oz corned beef
	$\frac{5}{8}$ oz of ordinary chocolate of $\frac{3}{4}$ oz of soluble
	$\frac{3}{4}$ oz of condensed milk
	$\frac{3}{8}$ oz of tea
Every 4 days	1 oz of salt
Weekly	$\frac{1}{2}$ oz of mustard
	$\frac{1}{4}$ oz of pepper
	$\frac{1}{4}$ pint of vinegar

[6] Hammock cords.

Daily   ¾ lb fresh meat
                          1 lb of vegetables.

('Report of the Committee into Canteen and Victualling
arrangements in H.M. Fleet', in *Parliamentary Papers*,
Vol. 50, 1907)

This committee on canteens and victualling, which reported in
1907, recommended other important changes, including a smaller
standard ration with less bread and meat, but an allowance of 4*d.* a
day, which each mess could spend on the food it liked. It also
recommended that fresh milk should be served in shore establishments, and that the old, hard, dry ship's biscuit, on which thousands
of sailors throughout the centuries must have cracked so many teeth,
should only be served in absolute emergencies.

There were many other improvements in the sailor's life, too. In
1857 a uniform, for which sailors had pleaded for so long, was
introduced.

My Lord Commissioners of the Admiralty have been pleased to establish
the following Regulations, for a uniform Dress for the Petty Officers,
Seamen and Boys in the Royal Navy....

  1. Blue Cloth Jacket...to be made of Navy Blue Cloth, double-
     breasted ... with ... seven Black Horn Crown and Anchor Buttons
  2. Blue Cloth Trousers ...
  3. Duck or White Drill Frock ...
  4. Duck Trousers
  5. Blue Serge Frock
  6. Pea jacket[7]
  7. Black silk Handkerchief
  8. Hat. To be black or white according to climate ... with a hat ribbon
     bearing the ship's name
  9. Cap to be worn at night, and at sea when ordered
  10. Woollen comforter to be of dark blue colour....

(Admiralty Circular, No. 283, January 30, 1857)

The blue frock or blouse had a large, wide collar, on which three
rows of white tapes were sewn, but there is no evidence to support the
popular belief that these commemorated Nelson's three major victories over the French. (French sailors have the same ornamental
tapes, too!)

[7] Loose jacket of coarse woollen material.

The Admiralty still kept a firm hand on its sailors, but the severity of former times was gradually mitigated. Flogging was never officially abolished in the Navy. As late as the 1840s it was still a common weekly spectacle on some ships, and men were still being sentenced by courts-martial to be flogged round the fleet. But flogging declined after annual returns of punishments in the Navy had to be presented to Parliament in the early 1850s, though even in 1862 over a thousand sailors were flogged. By 1878, however, there were only two cases, and the last flogging took place in 1880. For a number of years, however, boys continued to be birched or caned—312 in 1878.

As a substitute for these savage punishments, the Navy opened its own prison in Lewes, Sussex, in 1862, where the worst offenders were confined in rigorous conditions.

> The naval prison will contain about one hundred and twenty men in solitary confinement. . . .
>
> In going through the establishment, we are struck with the good order and dead silence that prevail, broken only by the monotonous voice of the warder conducting the shot-drill.[8]
>
> A part of the system which affects the smart-looking men most is the rule under which the hair of all prisoners is cut close to the head every fortnight. . . .
>
> The royal navy and marine forces number sixty thousand men and out of this number . . . five hundred annually are committed to the naval prison.
>
> (Anon: 'The Naval Prison at Lewes', *Chambers's Journal*, 6th June 1874)

Other men were sentenced to penal servitude in civilian prisons, dismissed from the Service, or confined to cells on board ship. But by the end of the century most of the offences and punishments were minor ones.

> The system of punishment results in nearly all the dirty and disagreeable work of the ship being done in expiation of misdemeanours. . . . Occasionally a youngster will be sentenced to a few strokes on the breech with a cane. . . .
>
> Offences are now mostly trivial, and almost confined to the younger members of the ship's company. . . .
>
> (Frank T. Bullen, op. cit.)

[8] The men carried a 32 lb shot waist-high for several yards, put it down, picked up another shot, and went on round in an unending circle.

The sailor benefited in many other ways in the new Navy. Shore leave of 48 hours could be granted by a captain from the early years of the century, and many of them did grant this. From 1890, it was given unconditionally to all sailors every three months unless they had committed some offence. There were better chances of promotion on the lower deck, too, with the institution of a new rating of leading seamen and a new class of petty officer in 1853. Pensions were also provided for those on long-term engagements, and as a result the Royal Hospital for living-in pensioners at Greenwich was closed in 1869. The low rates of basic pay, however, continued to be a source of grievance. The able seaman who got 1s. 2d. a day in 1829 received only 1s. 8d. a day in 1912, when he was given an extra 3d. a day after six years' service. But he could also get extra pay for good conduct and specialist training, and he was now at least paid regularly in cash, instead of receiving a wage ticket, which he had often had to sell at a loss.

3

In spite of increasing competition from other nations, Britain retained her supremacy as a naval Power right up to the First World War. In 1889 she adopted a two-power standard, under which she tried to keep the Royal Navy at a strength equivalent to that of any two other major nations combined—in battleships and cruisers. This

Part of the Home Fleet on exercises in 1907.
Imperial War Museum

standard was maintained for a number of years, but it could not be entirely adhered to in the naval arms race which followed the launching of the *Dreadnought* in 1906. Nevertheless, the Royal Navy was still the strongest in the world when the First World War broke out. It had 58 battleships of all kinds, against 35 German, 30 American, 21 French, 17 Japanese, 14 Austro-Hungarian, and 8 Russian. In the past it had defeated the Spanish, the Dutch and the French and now it was prepared to meet the even more menacing challenge from the new enemy—Germany.

4

1826	Stokers introduced in Navy
1827	Battle of Navarino Bay, last great battle under sail
1830	French occupation of Algerian ports curbs piracy
1853	Continuous service introduced in Navy
1856	Privateering ends in most countries
1857	Naval uniform introduced
1861	First ironclad, the *Warrior*, launched
1862	Naval prison opens at Lewes
1867	Naval rations increased
1869	Royal Hospital, Greenwich, closes
1880	Last flogging
1889	Britain adopts two-power standard
1890	Shore leave given every three months
1897	Parsons tests steam turbine
1901	First British submarine
1906	*Dreadnought* launched
1907	Rations improved

For Further Reading
Michael Lewis, *The Navy in Transition, 1814–1864*, Hodder and Stoughton, 1965

Part Six

The Merchant Service

1

With the exception of the large new steamship companies, the merchant service was much slower than the Royal Navy to adapt to the changed conditions of the modern age. As in former times, wages remained higher on merchant ships than in the Navy, and discipline was also less strict. But conditions aboard merchant vessels were generally dirtier; the work was often harder; and unscrupulous shipowners' neglect of safety caused a mounting loss of life among both seamen and passengers.

With the massive unemployment after the Napoleonic wars and the discharge of thousands of seamen from the Royal Navy, it was easy enough to find crews. Many of the masters under whom they served were drunken, vicious men, incompetent in both seamanship and navigation, and concerned only with cheating the crews out of as much money as they could. British consuls overseas were inundated with complaints from seamen who had been badly treated. Beatings, non-payment of wages and stranding in foreign ports were the most common complaints in the 1830s.

> His Britannic Majesty's Consulate,
> New York.
> John Davis, a British seaman, personally appeared before me . . . and doth declare and say, that he shipped as a cook on board the barque *Lady of the Lake*, of Glasgow, Robert White, master. . . . That having arrived at New York, and being unwell, deponent was, upon the application of said master to this office, sent to hospital near the city. That while there, the said Robert White departed from the port of New York, leaving deponent

in hospital, and carried away deponent's clothes, whereby he is obliged to resort to His Majesty's Consul for necessary clothing and bedding. . . .

Sworn before me this 17th day of July, 1834,
James Buchanan.
('Copies or Extracts relating to complaints of the
Discharge of British Seamen in Foreign Ports',
in *Parliamentary Papers*, 1835, Vol. 48)

Although many seamen were stranded by their masters, it was just as common—if not more common—for seamen to desert their ship in a foreign port, leaving the master stranded, without a crew to sail it back home again. Sometimes they deserted because they had been badly treated, but more often it was because they were persuaded to do so by some dishonest crimp. Crimps were touts for seamen's boarding-houses. They let the seamen have a few nights out on credit, visiting local outfitters, bars and prostitutes, and then doped them, or made them drunk, and put them on another ship, stealing their advance of wages.

At this period 'crimping' was one of the worst features of Quebec; and nothing seemed to check it. No matter how closely a ship was watched, crimps and boarding-house runners would always find a means of getting on board. By their persuasive powers, assisted by a bottle of 'chain-lightning' (a spiritous compound that has the dire effect of stealing the men's senses away), they generally managed to induce one or more to desert. The bait was the high rate of wages paid to seamen at the port, which was something like £12 to £14 per month. In many cases the whole crew would clear out in one night, often leaving three and four months' pay behind them. For what? They might be ashore for two or three days—rarely more, and often less. The boarding-masters would see that they were well plied with liquor. In the majority of cases they would only come to their senses under the influence of a splitting headache, to find themselves in a strange ship, and halfway down the St. Lawrence on their way to Europe, after having had an advance of wages that would probably cover all they would earn on the passage. Out of this, looking through their effects, they might find they had a dozen boxes of matches, a bar of soap, and perhaps an oilskin coat thrown in. . . .

Of course the boarding-masters reaped the benefit of Jack's folly and short-sightedness. . . . The whole of the crew, with the exception of the officers and myself, were finally induced to desert, leaving behind their four months' pay.

(William R. Lord: *Real Life at Sea, being the reminiscences
of a Sailor*, London, 1913)

Seamen at work on the after-deck of the passenger ship *Asia*.
Mansell Collection

Life aboard sailing-ships in the nineteenth century remained almost as hard as it had ever been for both the crew and the passengers.

The watch on deck is...rather alcoholic, but it has put on its dreadnoughts,[1] tarpaulins, oilskins, and sea-boots, put up its collars, pulled down its sou'westers, lighted its pipes, cut its quids, and is taking 'fishermen's walks—two steps and overboard', upon the sloppy deck. The crew is miscellaneous—English, Scotch, Irish, Welsh, American, Dutch, Danish, Swedish, Spanish, mulatto, Jewish, and 'cornstalk'.[2] The cook's mate, a dirty old fellow, who wears a brimless hat like an inverted inkstand, says that he was once the editor of an influential journal....

The deck leaks; in forecastle and in 'tween decks, here and there in the saloon, too, sleepers are roused from their slumbers by dirty water

[1] Thick coat worn in stormy weather.
[2] Australian.

trickling down their noses, or drip-drip-dripping into their open mouths. The ship shudders and shrinks as if she had been stung, and creaks like a crushed basket as billow after billow thumps against her bow like a battering ram and deluges her deck with a curving shower of spray. . . . The cow and the sheep are ousted from their quarters and make a plaintive clamour as they stagger about disconsolate. . . .

The wheel wrenches itself out of the hands of the two steersmen, and spins round like a catherine-wheel. . . . Slushy snow lies in deep drifts on the lee side of the decks . . . and is shaken out of the belly of each flapping sail. Icicles a foot long, bristling like bayonets, hang from the eaves of the deck houses. Pulleys and sheaves are frozen fast together, and hot water has to be poured on the blocks before the rigging will run. Some of the crew have their fingers frost-bitten; all come off their watch with their beards and whiskers frozen silverily bright and hard.

(Richard Rowe: *Jack Afloat and Ashore*, London, 1875)

In spite of all the hardships, there were some men—masters, perhaps, more than crews—who were reluctant to change sail for steam. As the days of the sailing-ship drew to a close there were many who looked back with some sentimentality to the vanishing glories of the age of sail; and by the end of the century some apologists were already trying to invest the sailor's life with an ease and comfort that it never did possess.

I come now to the questions of hardships which sailors occasionally experience in following their vocation. These are, at times, undoubtedly severe; yet upon being looked into, they do not, perhaps present that appalling aspect so generally associated with a seaman's life. Jack's duties are well regulated . . . . Out of twelve hours' deck duty he has only six hours' actual work . . . such as repairing the rigging, painting, splicing etc. During the remaining six hours of his watch on deck, he is only called upon when sails require to be taken in or set, or yards trimmed. In fine weather sails are frequently not touched for days, nor are the yards. His duties at such times are, therefore, light, for during the night watches Jack coils himself up on deck or lies down with his clothes on in his bunk, and sleeps as soundly as though he were on a feather bed at home.

(H. E. Acraman Coate: *Realities of Sea Life*, London, 1898)

In some ways, however, this reluctance to give up sail was understandable. At the very moment when sail was about to be almost entirely superseded, a completely new kind of sailing-ship was developed. The clipper, an American invention of the 1820s, was a large ship for those days, built for speed, with a long, sleek hull, and tall, raked masts crowded with sail. At times clippers logged a speed of over 20 knots. They were first used in the opium trade, to China, and then, after the repeal of the Navigation Acts in 1849, for rushing cargoes of tea from China to Britain. From the middle of the 1850s, Britain started to build clippers of her own, which were smaller but faster than the American ships. Helped by the decline of the American mercantile marine during the Civil War, 1861–5, British clippers swept their rivals off the seas. These ships made the journey from Foochow in ninety days or so, but by the time the British clipper had been developed to such perfection the necessity for it had already gone. By the 1860s improved steamships, which could do the journey in sixty-five days, had been developed. Clippers could not compete.

About this time a big steamboat went past us with a cheer, and headed out to meet the blast. A sailing vessel could not get out with this wind.

We could see that the other vessels had also made preparation to weather the gale at their moorings, and a few that were in ballast jumped and tossed like a switch-back.

The clear sky did not last long, however; heavy squalls drove over and covered the stars and moon with inky blackness, and then a heavy moan, as if of distant thunder, and then the blast burst with hurricane fury.

We rolled and plunged and tore at our cables like a mad horse at his tether. . . .

At about ten o'clock the vessel gave a violent plunge and buried her head under a cataract of waters. Then she suddenly rose, and with water streaming from her sides she mounted up, bow first, into the air. A sudden strain was thus placed on the cables, and the heavy capstan . . . was torn from its fittings and hurled over the side as if it had been a toy.

Presently a rocket flew upwards and rent the darkness of the night—a signal of distress from a vessel driving on the beach from her anchors. . . . A vessel saw her signal, and, though in great danger herself, lowered her life-boat and saved two-thirds of her crew. . . .

At last the morning dawned, but the ashen hues of dawn broke on a cheerless scene; and when the wind lulled we found that six ships had gone ashore, and the gale was responsible for the loss of about sixty lives. (Ernest Richards: *In a Deep Water Ship, A Personal Narrative of a Year's Voyage as an Apprentice in a British Clipper Ship*, London, 1907)

The clippers, and other sailing-vessels, gained a new lease of life for a few decades more on the routes to Australia and New Zealand. Many of them took out emigrants and then—after the bunks between decks had been ripped out—returned with a cargo of wool.

Our passengers were sent off to us in tenders. What a crowd they were! Scotch, Irish, Welsh, every denizen of the British Isles was represented,

Between decks on an emigrant ship.
National Maritime Museum

not one in a hundred perhaps ever having seen a ship before, and as Jack quaintly remarked, 'You could see the hay seed still in their hair'. . . . All these bound for New Zealand, 'the working man's paradise'. After the tedious job of getting them under hatches was finally accomplished . . . sail was made, and with our human freight we stood away to the south'ard. . . .

The emigrants had by this time settled down to the ship life, and were as happy and comfortable as possible, and well they might be, most of them never having fed so decently in their lives before. . . . In comparison with the sailors, they lived like aldermen . . . soft bread and tinned vegetables in plenty being served out to them every day, often looked upon with envious eyes by the crew. . . .

We had been running with a westerly wind behind us which gradually freshened and increased, bringing up a long roll of a sea that plainly indicated that there was yet something heavier behind it. Harder and harder blew the wind, and higher and higher became the sea, until we were scudding before it. . . .

The emigrants were not enjoying life at this time . . . with the advent of bad weather having been battened down below for the last two days. In spite of ventilators, under these conditions, with between three and four hundred human beings under decks, anything but salubrious was the atmosphere....

It was the magic cry of 'Land oh!' some weeks later that quite restored again the usual cheerfulness to the ship. Everything else was forgotten but the patent fact, the land of promise was in sight. As it became more distinct, the excitement among the emigrants grew in proportion. Mothers held their children up, fondly hoping to draw their attention to the land of their adoption....

We were bound for Lyttletown and ... quite a number of open boats might be seen coming out to meet us....

At this time the sailing ship was the only means of transport between the old country and New Zealand.... The arrival of a ship was a red-letter day, and a matter of interest to half the town, for mostly she carried a living freight, to cultivate and people the land.

(Charles Protheroe: *Life in the Mercantile Marine*, John Lane, The Bodley Head, 1903)

The most famous clipper of all, the *Cutty Sark*, 963 tons, (now thankfully preserved at Greenwich as a unique memorial to a vanished age) was one of the fastest vessels in the Australian wool trade. Launched at Dumbarton on the Clyde in 1869, she brought back tea from China until 1877; three years later she carried her first cargo of wool from Australia, and her last in 1895. In that year, she was sold to Portuguese owners, and as the *Ferreira* of Lisbon roamed the seas in search of cargo until she was bought by an English captain in 1922. Just before the First World War, a Merchant Navy officer had happened to spot the *Cutty Sark* in the port of New Orleans.

The sun, high in the heavens, shone down with a dazzling glare on her weather-beaten hull, painfully emphasising every detail of its shabby exterior and general air of neglect, but though shorn of much of her former glory the unmistakable stamp of an aristocrat of the sea was ineradicable. It shone forth despite her tattered gear and pitted bulwarks. Like the old racer one sometimes sees relegated to the 'shafts', the breed was unmistakable....

Wondering vaguely what old clipper she might be, I sauntered along the wharf admiring her graceful lines....

For a figure-head she had a comely maiden with swelling bosom and hand outstretched pointing ahead—plentifully bedaubed with multi-coloured paint. Though in hopes of finding some trace of her old name on the bows, I searched in vain—everything was obliterated and only the glaring *Ferreira* remained.... Walking over the gangway, I made my way slowly aft and mounted the poop.

To give the dagoes credit, they certainly did devote a little attention to this part of the ship though occasional startling splashes of colour (so dear to the Portuguese) struck a jarring note. The upper poop consisted of a raised deckhouse, some $3\frac{1}{2}$ feet high. It was neatly railed and hammock-netted round. Along the port and starboard sides ran a row of garden seats.

(Quoted in Basil Lubbock: *The China Clippers*, Glasgow, 1914)

Sailing-ships were doomed. Even without competition from steam-ships it would have become increasingly difficult to find a sufficient number of men to sail them. With the improvements in conditions of life ashore, fewer men were willing to tolerate the hardships of life at sea, and many shipowners were forced to look abroad for their crews.

The growth of trade, and the consequent additional opportunities for employment on shore, as well as at sea, have increased the difficulty of obtaining able seamen. The wages of seamen have risen largely within the last few years, but yet shipowners complain that they are often compelled to take such men as present themselves, of whom many prove to be incompetent to discharge properly the duties of seamen. The ignorance and incapacity of these men throw additional work on the good seamen, cause dissatisfaction in the ship, and enhance the dangers of naviga-tion. . . .

The general tendency of the evidence . . . leads to the conclusion that there is a deficiency of British able seamen; captains of merchant vessels could not, it is said, man their vessels without Swedes, Norwegians, and Lascars.

(Final Report, Royal Commission on Unseaworthy Ships, in *Parliamentary Papers*, 1874, Vol. 34)

This tendency to employ foreigners, with fewer opportunities for employment in their own country, increased as the century pro-gressed. In 1880 over 13 per cent of seamen in British ships were foreigners; by 1903 this percentage had reached a peak of nearly 23 per cent. Thereafter, the proportion started to decline, as improve-ments in conditions and pay started to attract more British recruits again.

Even in the days of sail there had always been a number of shipowners and companies offering relatively good conditions of employment to their crews. One was the East India Company, which, however, lost its last monopoly of trade to the East in 1834, when most of its ships were sold, and was finally abolished in 1858. The high traditions of the company were continued by the Blackwall Frigates, which sailed to India and Australia. But, on the whole, it was only after the development of the big steamship companies that conditions

Furniss: Coloured seamen washing the decks on a passenger ship.
P & O Shipping Line

for merchant seamen started to improve, and even then not without a
long struggle by the men's union.

Steam-vessels had first been developed for use on canals, rivers and
lakes.[3] In the 1820s their use began in the coastal trade, and in the
Irish Sea and the English Channel. In 1826 the General Steam
Navigation Company, which had been founded two years before,
introduced them on the England–Portugal route. It was not until
1838 that the British paddle-steamer *Sirius* became the first steamship to cross the Atlantic unaided by sail. She was followed into New
York harbour twelve hours later by Isambard Kingdom Brunel's
Great Western. After that developments were more rapid, with the
formation of the big steamship companies which were increasingly to
dominate mercantile affairs for the remainder of the century.

The first steamers were used mainly for carrying passengers; they
received a hidden Government subsidy by being given contracts to
carry overseas mail, which by 1860 amounted in all to £1m a year.
The Cunard line was awarded the contract to carry the Atlantic mail

[3] For these developments see pp. 11–26 in a companion volume by the present
author, *Travel and Communications,* Harrap, 1972.

in 1839; the Peninsular and Oriental shipping company was given the Indian contract in the following year; and the Royal Mail Steam Packet Company was awarded the West Indian contract in 1841.

The first steamships were small, wooden vessels, equipped with paddle-wheels and auxiliary sails: the *Sirius* was only 703 tons. It was impossible to build wooden ships with a hull of more than about 300 feet. But with the introduction of iron ships (the first small iron ship, the *Aaron Manby*, which was 120 feet long, was launched in 1821) much bigger vessels could be built. One of the first men to see the possibilities was that versatile genius, Brunel, who designed the *Great Eastern*, of 18 915 tons. It was nearly 700 feet long and 83 feet in beam, had both screw propellers and paddle-wheels, and was designed to carry 4 000 passengers to the United States in seven days and to Australia in thirty-five. It was launched in 1858, after an attempt to launch it in the previous year had failed because of its huge size. Although it was a commercial failure, it was far ahead of its time, and was not surpassed in size for nearly forty years.

Brunel's *Great Britain* which is now on show at Bristol.
South West Picture Agency, Bristol

S.S. GREAT BRITAIN

The saloons are 60 feet in length, the principal one nearly half the width of the vessel, and lighted by skylights from the upper deck. On either side are the cabins and berths.... The berths of the crew are forward, below the forecastle.... Below the berths of the seamen are two enormous cavities for cargo; of which 5,000 tons can be carried, besides coals enough for the voyage to Australia, making about as many tons more.... The screw engines, designed and manufactured by Messrs. James Watt and Co., are by far the largest ever constructed; and ... will exert an effective force of not less than 8,000 horses.... The funnels, of which there will be five, are constructed with double casings ... filled with water ... preventing the radiation of heat to the decks.... The captain's apartment is placed amidships, immediately below the bridge; whence the electric telegraph will flash the commander's orders to the engineer below, helmsman at the wheel, and look-out man at the bows.

(*The Annual Register*, London, 1857)

By 1870 five-sixths of all new ships were being built of iron, and by the end of the century, with the introduction of cheaper steel-making processes, iron had been almost entirely replaced by steel. Steam-engines were improved, too; John Elder's more efficient compound engine, successfully tested in 1854, meant that less coal had to be carried, leaving room for more cargo. Alfred Holt's even more economical engine was first tried out in 1862. By that time, too, paddle-wheels had been replaced by a screw propeller. In the 1880s auxiliary sails—which were still carried in case the propeller shaft broke—were abandoned, with the installation of twin screws. The steamship's greater size and power meant that more cargo could be carried, with greater certainty of arriving at a specified time. But the triumph of steam was a slow process in the merchant service. Even by 1874 there were still 20 766 British sailing-ships, including fishing-vessels, and only 4 343 steamers: it was not until the middle of the 1880s that the total of steam tonnage exceeded that of sail for the first time.

From the beginning of the present century, there was an increasing specialization in steamships, with small tramp steamers roaming the oceans of the world in search of cargo; mixed cargo and passenger ships; and the large new luxury liners, like the *Mauretania,* of 31 000 tons—the pride of the Cunard line. Launched in 1907 and fitted with steam turbines, *Mauretania* was capable of maintaining a speed of 24 to 25 knots in moderate weather. She held the 'blue riband' for the Atlantic crossing from 1909 to 1930.

Steamship lines were able to attract, and to keep, better crews because the regularity of their sailings enabled them to offer continuous employment to seamen, as the Navy had done for sailors since 1853.

The coasting trade, and some of the great lines of steamers, attract the steadiest and best seamen. Voyages in which men are not long absent from home, and where vessels return periodically to the same port, are naturally preferred. The wages, the accommodation, and the food, are generally better in the large steamers.

(Royal Commission on Unseaworthy Ships, op. cit.)

Wages in steamships by the end of the century tended to be about 10s. to 25s. higher per month than in sailing vessels. The average menu for the week on sailing ships and tramp steamers at the end of the century was:

Water	3 quarts daily
Bread	1 lb daily
Beef	1½ lb Sunday, Tuesday, Thursday, Saturday
Pork	1¼ lb Monday, Wednesday, Friday
Flour	½ lb Sunday, Tuesday, Thursday
Peas	⅓ pint Monday, Wednesday, Friday
Rice	½ lb Saturday
Tea	⅛ oz daily
Coffee	½ oz daily
Sugar	2 oz daily
No spirits allowed	

(F. W. Gardner: *The Sea: A Guide*, London, 1902)

But the bigger steamships provided, in addition to these items, many others, including pickles, molasses, marmalade, jam, butter and dried fruit. Accommodation, though poor enough in some cases, was also an improvement on that to be found in many sailing-ships. Nevertheless, right up to the First World War—and in some cases beyond—the merchant seaman's life was by no means a happy one. From 1901 to 1912 the death-rate from disease alone among the crews of British merchant ships was 1 in 207 in the worst year and 1 in 269 in the best. (It was, of course, much higher on the land also than it is now.) In most years deaths were proportionately higher in steamships than in sailing-vessels: the firemen, or stokers, had one of the dirtiest and unhealthiest jobs, and on small tramp steamers their living conditions were unhygienic too.

We had better try to imagine the crew-space itself in 1894. It is a wedge-shaped space; the nose of the ship is itself a wedge; this is divided

Stokers firing the boilers on a merchant ship.
Imperial War Museum

by a central partition, and the sailors live on the starboard, stokers on the port side. It is some 6 feet 6 inches high, and is built of iron beams over which are spread iron plates. The space for twelve sailors would be 864 cubic feet or less (a third-class railway compartment is about 266 cubic feet. . . .) The place will be painted yellow . . . and will be dark because the windows are so small. Then there are the berths, twelve of them probably of wood, arranged in pairs (even threes!) above one another. . . . . Under the berths, or in corners are the men's bags, any other personal property being stored in their beds. . . . They have only buckets to wash in, and their bedding and clothes are dirty too, for they have no seats but the shelf mentioned, so when they are tired they lie at once down on their beds in their boots, firemen off watch in their engine-room clothes; and, by the bye, the privy is closely adjacent and likely adds its aroma. . . . It is hand flushed, choked very likely, and like the stove, being no one's particular care, it is neglected; it has no flush but a bucket, and is out of action.

In the crew space there is no table, there is no chair, there is no spare space, no cupboard or locker for clothes, nowhere to hang up an overcoat to dry. By the way, all meals are taken here, and at sea some cooking is done on the stove, as it is so hard to get any meal from the galley over the wave-swept upper deck.

(W. E. Home: *Merchant Seamen, their diseases and their welfare needs,* John Murray, 1922)

Disease was not the only killer. Every year hundreds of lives were lost in shipwrecks, fires, collisions, or in ships which just disappeared without a trace.

> According to Mr. Gray, the Assistant Secretary of the Board of Trade, the average number of men employed in vessels registered in the United Kingdom was from 210,000 to 217,000 and the proportion of men who lost their lives in wrecks or other casualties . . . varied from 1 in 81 in 1875 to 1 in 56 in 1883.
> (Final Report, Royal Commission on the Loss of Life at Sea, in *Parliamentary Papers*, 1887, Vol. 43)

In the nineteenth century practically all merchant seamen had graphic tales to tell of the times they had been ship-wrecked.

> Rees is my name . . . I'm a Welshman, from Aberdowey, Merionethshire. . . . Three times I've been wrecked. First time was in 1831, in the brigantine 'Meredith' of Bristol, Captain William Frederick. She'd gone to Labrador to load fish back. It was on the 13th of November; about nine at night we found ourselves close to the breakers at Cape Luff, with the sails blowing away. We got into the boat with two pint bottles of rum, and two pint bottles of water. That's all we had—no food. We were twenty-four hours in the boat, and then we landed at Dead Island Harbour. Then we went south; we put in at Square Island and stayed there three days. . . . One of the poor chaps died, starved and frost-bitten. . . .
> (Richard Rowe, op. cit.)

It was not only sailing-vessels that were wrecked. Although passenger liners generally had a much better safety record, they also were lost. In 1866 a steamer on the way to Melbourne foundered in the Bay of Biscay with the loss of 220 lives. In the following year two steamers were driven ashore in a hurricane in the West Indies, and wrecked. In 1873 there were 300 people lost in a collision off Dungeness. While on its way to Cape Town in 1881, the *Teuton* struck on Quoin Point where another ship, the *Celt*, had been wrecked six years earlier. A terse telegraph message told the story of the disaster, in which over 230 lives were lost.

> At 9 p.m. boats lowered to rail and provisioned.
> At 10 p.m. water was over 'tween decks hatch in No. 2 hold; ship was stopped to lower boats; seven boats lowered; only one loaded women and

children, and two sailors; second boat commencing to load when ship foundered, at 10.50 p.m. sucking in everything. All compartments forward of engine-room filled. Engine-room free up to time of foundering, then supposed bulk-head burst and ship foundered instantly.

All those saved, except Lizzie Ross, Hirst and Walkenshaw, sank with ship and scrambled into boats afterwards.

Two boats reached Simon's Bay, one Table Bay. . . .

Captain at dinner when ship struck; thereafter remained on bridge until ship foundered.

Good discipline. No confusion. Passengers behaved splendidly.

(S. P. Oliver: *On Board a Union Steamer*, London, 1881)

But the disaster which, above all others, aroused the greatest public concern about safety at sea was the loss of the White Star liner *Titanic*, on the night of 14th April 1912. The largest ship then afloat, of 45 000 tons, with eight steel decks and watertight bulkheads, she was thought by many people to be unsinkable. But on her maiden voyage from Southampton to New York she struck an iceberg and sank less than three hours later, with the loss of over 1 500 crew and passengers, many of them prominent Americans.

There was some criticism among the survivors of the Titanic crew's inability to handle the lifeboats. 'The crew of the Titanic was a new one, of course,' declared Mrs. George N. Stone of Cincinatti, 'and had never been through a lifeboat drill, or any training in the rudiments of launching, manning and equipping the boats. . . . Had there been any sea running, instead of the glassy calm that prevailed, not a single passenger would have safely reached the surface of the water. The men did not know how to lower the boats; the boats were not provisioned; many of the sailors could not handle an oar with reasonable skill.'

Albert Major, steward of Titanic, admitted that . . . 'There had not been a single boat drill on the Titanic. The only time we were brought together was when we were mustered for roll call about nine o'clock on the morning we sailed. From Wednesday noon until Sunday nearly five days passed, but there was no boat drill.'

(Marshall Everett, editor: *Wreck and Sinking of the Titanic*, Chicago, 1912)

At the subsequent inquiry into the sinking it was revealed that there was only enough room in the lifeboats for half of the 2 200 passengers on board—and even that was double the legal requirement. As a result an international conference on safety at sea was held in the following year, and many others have been held since.

2

The enormous expansion of trade in the nineteenth century, when Britain was the major industrial nation and the Union Jack was flying in every continent, brought about an enormous expansion of shipping. Any man who could get hold of some kind of ship and some sort of crew and send it to sea stood a good chance of making a high profit. Some shipowners displayed such a reckless disregard for all safety that the Government was forced to intervene, and from about the 1830s there was scarcely a single year when some Government body was not investigating or reporting. Shipping losses captured the headlines then as aircraft crashes do nowadays.

In 1836 a Select Committee of the House of Commons was set up to inquire into the 'increasing number of shipwrecks', which had helped to bring the total number of lives lost at sea to 900 a year. Some astonishing evidence was given to the committee—of one ship that literally fell to pieces on her maiden voyage, of a master who had previously been a warehouse porter and had never before been to sea. The committee found that the main causes of these disasters were poorly built and badly maintained ships; excessive overloading of cargoes; and the drunkenness of seamen and the incompetence of officers.

The first major attempt to improve conditions at sea came with the passing of an Act in 1850, which set up a Mercantile Marine Department in the Board of Trade to supervise maritime affairs. Masters and mates of all foreign-going vessels had to pass an examination, and the master was also obliged to keep a ship's log while he was at sea. Discipline aboard ships was tightened up, with penalties being imposed for desertion, insubordination and any act that was likely to endanger the ship or its cargo. Many of these regulations were strengthened by the first merchant Shipping Act of 1854, which also gave the Board of Trade greater control over the supervision of ship construction, and made a number of improvements for the crews.

149. The Master of every Ship . . . shall enter into an Agreement with every Seaman . . . in a Form sanctioned by the Board of Trade . . . and shall contain the following Particulars. . . .
(1) The Nature, and, as far as practicable, the Duration of the intended Voyage or Engagement. . . .
(3) The Time at which each Seaman is to be on board or to begin work. . . .

(5) The Amount of Wages which each Seaman is to receive. . . .

(7) A Scale of Provisions which are to be furnished to each Seaman. . . .

224. The Master or Owner of every Foreign-going Ship (except those bound to European Ports or to Ports in the Mediterranean Sea . . .) shall also provide and cause to be kept on board such Ship a sufficient Quantity of Lime or Lemon Juice . . . and also of Sugar and Vinegar. . . .

The Master . . . shall serve out the Lime or Lemon Juice . . . and Sugar and Vinegar to the Crew, whenever they have consumed Salt Provisions for Ten Days, and so long afterwards as such Consumption continues, the Lime or Lemon Juice and Sugar daily at a Rate of Half an Ounce each per Day and the Vinegar weekly at the Rate of Half a Pint per week. . . .

231. Every Place in any Ship occupied by Seamen or Apprentices shall have for every such seaman or apprentice, if they sleep in Hammocks, a Space not less than Nine Superficial[4] Feet, and if they do not sleep in Hammocks, a space of not less than Twelve Superficial Feet. . . .

(*The Merchant Shipping Act*, London, 1854)

In spite of these regulations, there were over two hundred cases of scurvy, with six deaths, in merchant ships in 1878. There was also little real improvement in safety at sea. Masters put much of the blame for the increasing number of disasters on the drunkenness of crews.

Shipowners and captains of merchant ships concur in stating that a large portion of the ship's crew is very often brought or even lifted on board in a condition of helpless drunkeness, that the vessel must often be detained for twenty-four hours in order that the men may be so far recovered as to be able to get her under weigh.

(Royal Commission on Unseaworthy Ships, op. cit.)

Much of this drunkenness was caused by the lack of decent accommodation in ports, so that seamen became easy victims of dishonest crimps, who plied them with drugged drinks, and then shipped them aboard a vessel, and stole their advance of wages. During the century, a large number of charitable and religious organizations fought the crimps by providing better facilities for seamen ashore. In 1835 three naval officers founded a Sailors' Home near London Docks, which could accommodate 100 merchant seamen. Forty years later, there were twenty-eight similar homes in British ports and ten abroad.

Instead of . . . large dormitories . . . we find here long rows of little separate apartments, each of the inmates being allotted a small cabin big

[4] Square.

enough to contain his chest and 'kit', in addition to a clean and comfortable bed. This makes Jack feel quite at home, and as though he were on board ship. . . . In the dining room, four wholesome and substantial meals are furnished in the course of a day; and below-stairs is a 'bar', where beer and ale—undrugged—are supplied . . . as well as tea and coffee. There are baths and wash-houses and a barber's shop on the premises. . . . The moderate charge made . . . to boarders . . . is only fifteen shillings a week.

(Anon: 'Sailor's Home', in *Chambers' Journal*, 14th November 1874)

Many religious bodies, like the British and Foreign Sailors' Society, Missions to Seamen, the Seamen's Christian Friend Society and others, provided seamen not only with Bibles and tracts, but also with recreational facilities.

The British and Foreign Sailors' Society has its head-quarters in . . . the well-built Sailors' Institute, Mercers Street, Shadwell, just off the notorious Highway. It comprises a reading and writing room, a coffee room furnished with chess and draught boards, an excellent navigation school, a savings' bank, a depot for the sale of Bibles etc., and two lecture halls for . . . services and total abstinence lectures and meetings. The society has altogether twenty-five home and four foreign stations. . . .

(Richard Rowe, op. cit.)

But drunkenness was by no means the sole cause of disasters at sea. Many politicians and statesmen were engaged in the struggle to force shipowners to make their vessels safer. One of the prime causes was over-insurance, so that even if a ship was lost the owner received more in compensation than his ship was worth. As President of the Board of Trade, Joseph Chamberlain denounced the minority of shipowners who were engaged in the 'reckless pursuit of unholy gain'. There were many other causes, too: the lengthening of ships; deficient engine-power; defective construction; lack of repairs; undermanning; and overloading. Of all the politicians involved in the fight for greater safety at sea it was Samuel Plimsoll, the London coal merchant and M.P. for Derby, who most captured the public's imagination with his emotive appeals.

In this house, No. 9, L———ll Street, lives Mrs. A———r R———e. Look at her; she is not more than two- or three-and-twenty, and those two little ones are hers. She has a mangle, you see. It was subscribed for by her poor neighbours—the poor are very kind to each other. That poor little fellow has hurt his foot, and looks wonderingly at the tearful face of his young mother. She had a loving husband but very lately; but the owner of the ship, the S————n, on which he served, was a very needy man, who had insured her for nearly £3,000 more than she had cost him; so, if she sank, he would gain all this. Well, one voyage she was loaded *under the owner's personal superintendence;* she was loaded so deeply that the dock master pointed her out to a friend as she left the dock, and said emphatically, "that ship will never reach her destination." She never did, but was lost with all hands, twenty men and boys. . . .

(Samuel Plimsoll: *Our Seamen: An Appeal*, London, 1873)

Plimsoll has gone down in history as the man who did most to make shipping safe, and his name is commemorated in the load line, or Plimsoll mark, which all merchant ships were required to have on their hulls, after the passing of the Merchant Shipping Act in 1876. The line shows the depth to which the vessel can be safely loaded. But it is sometimes forgotten that the famous Plimsoll mark was almost totally ineffective for the first twenty-four years, as shipowners were allowed to put it where they liked: it was not until 1890 that it had to be approved by the Board of Trade. Moreover, other causes of disaster, such as excessive deck-loading, continued well into the present century.

The seamen themselves, who really knew just how bad conditions were afloat, and suffered most from them, also took an increasing part in the fight for improvements. A National Sailors' and Firemen's Union was formed in 1887 by Joseph Havelock Wilson, who first went to sea as a boy in 1871 and later opened a restaurant in Sunderland. He conducted a ceaseless campaign to improve wages, reduce hours of work, and make the seamen's voice heard in Parliament. Because of the use of cheap foreign labour, seamen's wages could be kept low. In 1900 they ranged from £3 to £4 a month, plus food.

In 1911 Wilson called his men out on strike, demanding a basic wage of £6 a month on passenger liners, £5 10s. on cargo ships and 35s. a week on coasters. When the owners tried to bring in blacklegs the dockers came out in sympathy, and the country's ports were at a standstill. Within a fortnight the seamen had won their fight and most shipowners had agreed to a substantial increase in wages.

Looking back over his campaigns later, Wilson could feel quite satisfied with the results.

My policy and the aims and ideals of the union have secured for the toilers of the sea conditions and a measure of freedom and liberty that is hardly realised by most people. It is not too much to say that the improvements secured since the bad old days, when I first went to sea, are no less than a revolution.

It seems a long time since the reform was won of abolishing the payment by seamen for the contract to work, when one shilling had to be paid by the men when they signed on a ship and another shilling when they signed off. This was no great injustice in days of sailing ships, when voyages lasted two or three years, but with the coming of steamships, doing so many as eight and more voyages each year, it meant a tax on seamen of sixteen shillings and more per year.

Long is the list of other improvements and reforms.

We secured the passing of regulations to ensure that seamen would have more safety whilst serving on vessels, and statistics show that by comparing the loss of life at sea today as compared with thirty years ago the difference is most marked; I do not claim this as being entirely due to restrictive legislation—a good deal of the losses being prevented by the difference of construction of vessels, their size and that important invention, the wireless.

(J. Havelock Wilson: *My Stormy Voyage through Life*, London, 1925)

3

In the nineteenth century British merchant ships dominated the oceans of the world. In the days of sail the mercantile marine was faced with strong competition from the Americans and their clippers. But the linking of the east and west coasts of the United States by rail diminished American interest in shipping. Towards the end of the century, in the era of the great luxury liners, Britain had to face a new challenge, just as the Navy did, from Germany: by 1914 the Hamburg–American passenger line was the biggest single shipping enterprise in the world.

Meanwhile, however, the British merchant service had become in total by far the largest of all. Britain had quite different interests from either the United States or Germany. She needed ships to communicate with, and to carry goods to and from, her vast empire, which at its peak covered about one-fifth of the total land area of the world. Her industry was dependent on the import of huge quantities of raw materials and the export of manufactured goods by sea. In addition it had to import food to feed its rapidly growing population.

The repeal of the Navigation Acts in 1849 revitalized the industry by ending the protection behind which British shipowners, with some

notable exceptions, had sheltered for so long. It had to improve its
ships, its services, if not its treatment of its crews, if it was to reap all
the rich benefits that these new opportunities presented. By 1900 the
Merchant Navy had reached a peak, with nearly 20 000 vessels of a
total tonnage of over 14 million registered in Britain—almost half the
total tonnage in the world.

4

1821	*Aaron Manby*, first iron ship, launched
1824	General Steam Navigation Company formed
1834	East India Company loses monopoly of trade to China (monopoly in India abolished in 1813)
1835	First Sailors' Home opened in London
1836	Select Committee on Shipwrecks
1838	*Sirius* first steamship to cross Atlantic, unaided by sail
1839	Cunard awarded Atlantic mail contract
1840	Peninsular and Oriental line gets Indian mail contract
1841	Royal Mail Steam Packet Company granted contract for West Indies mail
1849	Navigation Acts repealed, except for coasting trade, repealed in 1854
1850	Mercantile Marine Act introduces examinations for masters
1854	First Merchant Shipping Act
1856	John Elder's compound steam-engine
1858	East India Company abolished
1858	*Great Eastern* launched
1862	Alfred Holt's triple expansion engine
1874	Royal Commission on Unseaworthy Ships reports
1876	Plimsoll mark
1880's	Auxiliary sails abandoned; steam tonnage exceeds sail tonnage for the first time
1887	Royal Commission on Loss of Life at Sea reports
1887	National Sailors' and Firemen's Union formed
1907	*Mauretania* launched
1912	*Titanic* sinks

For Further Reading
Frank G. G. Carr: *The Cutty Sark and the Days of Sail*, Pitkin Pictorials, 1969
Hilda Kay Grant: *Samuel Cunard, Pioneer of the Atlantic Steamship*, Abelard-Schuman, 1967
David Masters: *The Plimsoll Mark*, Cassell, 1955

Part Seven

Total War

1

The merchant service and the Royal Navy had been separated in the nineteenth century, but they came together again in the exhausting struggle of two world wars against Germany, when British mastery of the seas prevented the country from being invaded or being starved into submission. Officers and men in the merchant service who were members of the Royal Naval Reserve, established in 1859, served with distinction in both wars. 'Landsmen' were also brought back to the decks of naval vessels with the introduction of conscription. And women played their part, too, taking over many shore jobs to release sailors for service at sea.

During the opening months of the First World War the main dangers to merchant shipping came from minefields and attacks by German cruisers, but the menace of German U-boats, or submarines, increased as the war went on. In February 1915 Germany announced that the sea around Great Britain would be regarded as a military area in which any British merchant ship would be attacked and destroyed. Few people believed that the Germans would carry out this threat in full by attacking unarmed passenger liners. But on 7th May 1915, without any warning, a German submarine sank the Cunard liner *Lusitania*.

At two o'clock on that Friday afternoon a couple of able seamen went up to relieve the men keeping a lookout in the crow's-nest on the foremast. One took the port side, the other the starboard side.

The man on the port side scanned the smooth bright sea and marked the coloured cliffs of the Irish coast showing through the haze. . . .

Said port to starboard, 'Anything in sight?'

To which starboard replied, 'Nothing doing.'

There was a few minutes' silence. Then starboard said to port:

'Good God, Frank, here's a torpedo!' And he shouted to the bridge below with all his strength.

Port, turning to his mate's side, perceived a white track lengthening swiftly from a spot some two hundred yards away from the ship. The next moment came an order from the bridge: 'All hands to boat stations,' and the men went down.

When the A.B. told his mate there was a torpedo coming, the master, standing outside the door of his room on the A deck, also saw the white track. The quartermaster at the wheel heard the second officer sing out, 'Here is a torpedo.' An able seaman on the saloon deck, looking through the port, saw a ripple on the water about 300 yards distant, then the white track, and then he saw the torpedo itself, and cried out a warning. . . .

The next moment another passenger, leaning over the rail, actually saw the torpedo strike the hull between the third and fourth funnels. He said the sound of the explosion was like a heavy door slammed by the wind.

The master, standing outside his room, was flung to the deck by the shock, and, picking himself up, ran to the navigation bridge. As he ran he felt a second explosion. The ship was already listing to starboard.

(L. Cope Cornford: *The Merchant Seaman in War*, Hodder and Stoughton, 1918)

Nearly 1 200 passengers, including over 120 Americans, and crew members lost their lives. This brutal act of aggression was one of the factors governing the United States' later entry into the war on the Allied side. As the war went on the menace of U-boats increased, reaching a peak in 1917, when the Germans adopted a policy of sinking all merchant ships at sight. The British replied with Q-boats—decoy vessels, disguised as small merchant ships, which waited for a U-boat to surface and then opened up with their hidden guns.

Towards the spring of 1917, however, the Hun began to get very wary, and for a 'Q' ship of any size it was almost imperative to take a torpedo; in other words to be torpedoed first. The ship was then 'abandoned', and the gun crews lay down upon the sinking vessel, trusting that the submarine would come to the surface to obtain information as to the vessel they had attacked, her cargo, the port she had left, and that to which she was bound. This, again, was an ideal opportunity for a 'Q' boat; but it required an iron discipline and self-restraint on the part of the captain, officers and crew to lie absolutely immobile upon a sinking vessel and await the coming of the submarine.

(Lt.-Commander Harold Auten: *'Q' Boat Adventures*, Herbert Jenkins, 1919)

The wreck of HMS *Invincible* in the Battle of Jutland.

Imperial War Museum

Although they gave some U-boats a nasty fright, and sank eleven of them, Q-boats were much less effective than the convoy system in beating the submarines.

The major naval encounter of the First World War came at the battle of Jutland. The British Grand Fleet under Admiral Jellicoe was stationed at Scapa Flow, in the Orkneys, and a force of battle cruisers at Rosyth. The German High Sea Fleet was based at Kiel. The reluctance of the Germans to come out and fight produced a great sense of frustration among many members of the British crew.

> The deadly monotony of the work of the Grand Fleet will probably never be fully realised by any but those whose fate it was to wait day after day, and week after week, for the longed-for encounter with the enemy. Only that ever-present hope carried us through that dreary second winter of the war. An occasional interval at sea for manoeuvres was the sole relief.

(Anon: *From Snotty to Sub*, Heinemann, 1918)

But eventually the Germans emerged and on 31st May 1916, the two main fleets of 28 British and 22 German battleships met. The British lost three battle cruisers, three cruisers and eight destroyers, the Germans, a battleship, a battle cruiser, four light cruisers and five destroyers. Petty Officer Francis, who was picked up by a destroyer later, relates how he narrowly escaped death after his battle cruiser, the *Queen Mary*, was sunk.

I clambered up over the slimy bilge keel and fell off into the water, followed, I should think, by about five other men.

I struck away from the ship as hard as I could, and must have covered nearly 50 yards, when there was a big smash, and stopping and looking round, the air seemed to be full of fragments and flying pieces.

(H. W. Fawcett and G. W. W. Hooper: *The Fighting at Jutland*, London, 1921)

A piece of timber floated in front of him, and with great exertion he managed to pull himself on top and then lost consciousness.

When I came to my senses again I was halfway off the spar, but managed to get back again. I was very sick, and seemed to be full up with oil fuel. My eyes were blocked up completely with it, and I could not see; I suppose the oil had got a bit dry and crusted. I managed, by turning back the sleeve of my jersey which was thick with oil, to expose a part of the sleeve of my flannel, and thus managed to get the thick oil off my face and eyes, which were aching awfully. Then I looked around, and seeing no one else, believed I was the only one left out of that fine ship's company. What had really happened was the *Laurel* had come up and picked up the remainder, and not seeing me lying on the spar had gone away out of the zone of fire, so how long I was in the water I do not know.

(Ibid.)

Dancing on deck in wartime.
Imperial War Museum

Although German losses at Jutland were lighter than the British, the High Seas Fleet never again emerged from the safety of its harbour, except for some minor sorties. During the First World War the Navy lost 312 warships of all types and over 22 000 officers and men.

The big shipping lines mobilized their vessels for war service.

At the outbreak of the war the Cunard fleet consisted of twenty-six sea-going steamers with a tonnage of some 330 000. Of these ships fifteen were lost, with two exceptions, by enemy action. . . . Cunard liners served as armed cruisers, transports, hospital ships and carried men, munitions and food to and from all parts of the world, steaming 3 500 000 miles. They transported just under one million soldiers and sailors, and over ten million tons of food stuffs and cargoes.

(Cunard Steamship Company: *On War Service*, 1919)

Dunkirk survivors returning to England.
Imperial War Museum

During the War the merchant service lost over 14 000 men from enemy action and over half of its total pre-War tonnage—7 800 000 tons in all.

In the Second World War there were no big naval battles between the British and the Germans, but a number of more isolated engagements, like the sinking of the German battleship, *Bismarck* in May 1941, and the scuttling of the pocket battleship *Graf Spee*, when it was trapped in the mouth of the river Plate by British cruisers in December 1939. In 1940, with the fall of France imminent, there was a naval operation unique in modern times, which with its combined force of warships and merchant vessels was in the old tradition stretching back to the defeat of the Spanish Armada. Every available ship and boat, including river pleasure steamers and small private craft, sailed over to Dunkirk, and between 27th May and 4th June successfully evacuated over 300 000 British and French soldiers, who had been cut off by the rapid German advance through the Low Countries and France. This is how the Dunkirk evacuation appeared to one regular stoker in a corvette.

The weather was good, the sea like a duck pond. As we approached Dunkirk it seemed as though all hell had broken loose. Soon we were amongst it all. Dive bombers were diving at us from everywhere, other fighter planes were strafing all around. . . .

As we got nearer inshore we could see thousands of troops on the beach, waiting in an orderly fashion to be picked up. Smaller boats were ferrying them from the beach to larger craft lying out in the harbour. The destroyers were doing a magnificient job, each going through heavy attacks to reach the jetty where they filled up quickly with soldiers. The enemy kept up a constant attack on them; it was a miracle anyone survived at all. At the same time the ships (including my own) kept up a terrific barrage. It didn't seem to deter the dive bombers in the least.

An old destroyer had a bomb go straight down her funnel and explode in the Boiler Room. It must have killed all personnel therein. . . .

So it went on night and day. As soon as my watch was finished I had to go straight to action stations. We would rush in to Sheerness, fill up with oil, stores and ammunition, and then out again. All the ship's company were getting worn out as we had no sleep. This was the hardest thing to go without. On arriving at our patrol area we would steam up and down. The ships continued to go to and fro in a never-ending line. Enemy aircraft played hell with them. They gave us a hectic time also. Luckily no serious damage occurred. . . .

We had lots of near misses, evading most of the bombs thanks to the splendid seamanship of the Captain, who swung the ship about like a mad thing.

We continued with this duty until June 4th, when the evacuation was completed. The weather had been very kind except for one night when it blew up a little. Had it not been for the good weather many more thousands of our troops would have been made prisoners.

(Frederick Wigby: *Stoker—Royal Navy*,
William Blackwood, 1967)

The aeroplane played a much bigger part in the Second World War than it had done in the first, with German reconnaissance aircraft reporting the position of merchant ships to patrolling German submarines, and German dive bombers attacking merchant vessels. A 29-year-old merchant seaman described in a broadcast talk, what it felt like when the dive bomber appeared.

And one evening, out of a clear sky, he'll come on you. You see him there, right up in the distance, a tiny little speck, and you whip out your binoculars and you look at him and you say, 'Now, what is it, what is it—is it a Lockheed, is it a Sunderland?' And you watch it, and suddenly an idea flashes across the back of your mind: 'My God! It is!' and you make one flying dive towards the Hotchkiss,[1] and you scream out 'Aircraft attack!'

Whip the covers off; she's loaded and ready. Get behind, he's coming down to you, he's coming down, and the noise is screaming and screaming, and you think to yourself, 'My God! He's coming for me, for *me!* for ME!' And you're standing there, and you can feel the sweat running down the backs of your knees. Then he gets closer and closer, and you can see those horrible splashes of the bullets as they come across the water and go ripping across the deck—and there's a noise like the opening of the gates of hell, and he's gone—and he's dropped his bombs—and he's missed you!

(Frank Laskier: *My Name is Frank*, Allen & Unwin, 1941)

Throughout much of the War the Navy's most fundamental task was to keep the vital Atlantic supply routes open for merchant ships. Thousands of sailors, seamen and troops who were being transported to distant theatres of war lost their lives. One nursing sister managed to escape with sixty-seven others in an open boat when their troop-ship was torpedoed off the coast of Africa.

Towards the end of our third week at sea, when I could no longer eat at all, because I was devoid of saliva, and depended for life on my water ration, we ran out of water. We had not sufficient for next day's ration. We prayed for rain. Next morning we had a torrential downpour, lasting

[1] Machine-gun.

nearly six hours. We caught it in every conceivable kind of vessel, as it ran from the sail, the gunwhale, the thwarts and the mast; and how we drank. Never had any of us seen or tasted anything so wonderful. . . .

We collected about six gallons of water in our tanks, which we kept. That which had run from the sail was dyed bright yellow, but who cared?
(Doris M. Hawkins: *Atlantic Torpedo*, Gollancz, 1943)

After travelling over seven hundred miles they landed on the coast of Liberia. Of the original sixty-eight in the boat, only sixteen survived. Thousands of others were to die before the Navy started to win the battle of the Atlantic in 1943, with the use of radar, long-range air patrols, aircraft carriers—the early ones being converted freighters—and more destroyers, some of them provided by the United States.

Passenger liners, including the two *Queens* of the Cunard line, again gave memorable service. The *Queen Elizabeth* of 82 998 tons, made her maiden voyage secretly to New York in 1940, and with her sister ship, the *Queen Mary*, of 81 237 tons, transported over 1½ million servicemen during the war. Losses of merchant ships were higher than in the First World War: over 2 600 British and Commonwealth ships, totalling nearly 11 400 000 tons, were destroyed. Casualties were higher, too, with nearly 30 000 seamen in British ships losing their lives—814 of them from fishing vessels.

The Navy expanded to an unprecedented size. By the end of the War there were 790 000 officers and men and 74 000 Wrens, and the total number of ships (including small vessels like landing craft) was 10 000. The Navy also had higher casualties, and over 50 000 men were killed.

2

The decline of international trade in the years between the two world wars affected merchant seamen more strongly than many other sections of the population. Immediately after the end of the First World War there was a great spurt in shipbuilding as owners replaced the vessels which had been destroyed by enemy action. But with the slump in trade, and increased competition from subsidized foreign lines, many ships were unable to get cargoes. In ports all over the country hundreds of tramp steamers were laid up; even the long-established shipping lines had a hard struggle to survive. Wages were cut by £2 10s. a month in 1921; masters and mates were glad to get work as able seamen. There was another shipping slump in 1929 to 1932, when one-fifth of the total tonnage was laid up. With this background, it is not surprising that there were few really major improvements in conditions in the mercantile marine.

Unlike the Royal Navy, the merchant service still had no uniform during the First World War. This sometimes led to embarrassing encounters with women who handed out white feathers to men who appeared to be dodging war service.

> During the war a fireman, torpedoed in his ship at sea, luckily got back to England and returned to his home at Southampton. As he and his mates walked out of Southampton West Station, in no characteristic uniform, they were met by a lady who presented to each of them—a white feather. 'Ma'am,' said my fireman . . . 'you can put that elsewhere; if it wasn't for me and other men like me, you'd be starving.'
>
> (Home, op. cit.)

A uniform was introduced after the end of the War, and in 1922 George V awarded the merchant service the title of Merchant Navy in recognition of its war-time heroism. A minimum scale of rations, which remained unchanged until 1939, had been laid down by the Merchant Shipping Act of 1906; it also provided that all ocean-going vessels should have a certificated cook aboard, and increased the minimum living space for each seaman to 120 cubic feet. Many of the large lines provided more than the minimum legal requirements for their crews, but a series of investigations by the *Lancet* in 1920 showed that there were still very great variations.

AQUITANIA

The sailors and firemen have small cabins, each holding three or four men. . . .

There were large mess-decks for the sailors and firemen, well warmed and well lighted, with tables for their food and benches to sit on.

All their food is drawn from the ship's galley, so the men do not have to prepare their own dinners. . . .

OLYMPIC

The sailors and the engine-room staff live forward in cabins, very like those of third-class passengers, but not all the beds are up to that quality, for there were several of the 'donkey's breakfast' pattern—beds stuffed with straw. Their cabins (each has in it a washing basin) generally berth three men; the three will rarely be there together. . . .

A FREIGHT LINER

This large freight liner had her crew on board. They lived forward and, as of old, the sailors (a dozen) on the starboard, the firemen (a score) on the port side—these latter rather more crowded. They had to reach their quarters over the bare iron deck, protected however by a top-gallant forecastle, and down a steep ladder, but when they got below they found themselves better off than in the old days, for a little space to make a lavatory and a mess-room had been on each side cut off the hold. . . .

As they were in the fore part of the ship, ventilation was scanty; the light was poor . . . and the atmosphere was stuffy, also damp. . . .

All water for use in the lavatory had to be carried from the galley.

(Quoted in Home, op. cit.)

In 1937 new minimum requirements were laid down: all ocean-going vessels of over 2 500 tons had to provide fully equipped mess rooms and bathrooms, and all accommodation had to be above the level of the load line.

The main grievance in the Navy in the inter-War period was over pay. In 1919 the basic pay of able seamen had been doubled to 4s. a day, plus many other allowances for kit, victualling and supporting their family. But in 1931, in the midst of an economic crisis, it was proposed to slash sailors' pay, in some cases by 25 per cent. The Atlantic fleet at Invergordon refused to put to sea, as the sailors at Spithead and the Nore had done over 130 years before. The Admiralty limited the pay cuts to 10 per cent, and the old rates of pay were restored in 1935, but the mutiny produced a discord which did not entirely disappear until the Second World War.

3

Although the Royal Navy remained a powerful force, and the merchant fleet remained very large, they had both lost the supremacy they had had in the nineteenth century. After the First World War the strength of the Royal Navy was limited by economic difficulties and the naval conference in Washington in 1921–2. At this international conference it was agreed that no new capital ships (battleships and battle cruisers) should be built for ten years, and that battleships then under construction should be limited in size to 35 000 tons. It was also agreed that the ratio of capital ships between Britain, the United States and Japan should be 5:5:3 respectively. The Royal Navy had fewer ships in 1939 than in 1914, and many of them were out of date; while Germany, which had been rearming even before Hitler came to power in 1933, had more modern ships and built up a huge force of U-boats soon after the War started.

The position of the Merchant Navy was also weakened by economic factors and greater foreign competition. Germany replaced its ships—confiscated at the end of the First World War—with the most up-to-date vessels. The United States built up a large merchant fleet during the War, and by 1922 had over 14 million tons. And other countries, particularly Japan, were increasing the size of their merchant fleets, too. Most foreign countries subsidized their shipping, as Britain had done in the 1840s, when so many of its major lines were established. But in the inter-War period it failed to do so, apart from a small subsidy for tramp steamers from 1935 to 1937. By 1939 Britain's merchant tonnage had declined to just over a quarter of the world's total.

4

1915	*Lusitania* sunk by U-boat
1916	Battle of Jutland
1919	Pay increase in Royal Navy
1921	Shipping slump; seamen's wages reduced
1921–2	Washington naval conference
1922	Title of Merchant Navy awarded by the King
1929–32	Second shipping slump
1930	London naval conference
1931	Invergordon mutiny
1939	*Graf Spee* scuttled
1940	Dunkirk evacuation
1940	*Queen Elizabeth's* maiden voyage
1941	*Bismarck* sunk
1943	Navy begins to win battle of the Atlantic

For Further Reading
Ronald Hope, editor: *Seamen and the Sea,* Harrap, 1965
J. P. W. Mallalieu: *Very Ordinary Seaman*, Gollancz, 1969

Part Eight

The Sailor—Today and Tomorrow

1

With advances in technology, ships have changed more radically since the last War than in the whole of the previous period covered in this book. The development of scheduled jet airline services since 1952, when the first was introduced by Britain, brought the era of the luxury passenger liner to a close after more than eighty years. The *Queen Mary* was sold to the city of Long Beach, California, for use as a floating hotel and convention centre in 1967; in the following year the *Queen Elizabeth* was also sold to the Americans for the same purpose. (Later it was resold to a Hong Kong shipping magnate, who planned to use it as a floating university, but it was destroyed by fire in 1972.) The *Queen Elizabeth 2*, of 65 863 tons, was launched in 1969, but like the few other similar super-luxury liners which have been built, it is intended more as a floating hotel, and cruise and holiday ship, than as a competitor with the airlines.

Even the general cargo ship no longer retains the importance that it once had, accounting for considerably less than one-half of the total deadweight tonnage (36 million) of Britain's merchant fleet in 1970. Apart from emergencies and storms—an unavoidable aspect still of life at sea—much of the life aboard a general cargo ship has become routine.

At sea the daily life of a ship pursues a routine of not unpleasant monotony. On the bridge, given decent visibility, there is little for the watch-keeping officer to do by day. . . . In the engine-room the engineers and greasers will be making their steady rounds of inspection and lubrication. On deck such hands as are not employed in the watch will be

A Petty Officer's Cabin on *Queen Elizabeth 2*.

Cunard

working under the bosun's orders at one or other of the manifold jobs of regular maintenance, inspecting and overhauling a lifeboat's gear, chipping and painting a derrick column, cleaning and oiling blocks and other tackle, polishing bright metal fittings, rigging a canvas bath or marking out a deck tennis court. In short, given decent food, reasonably fair weather and sociable ship-mates, the seafarer's day may be pleasantly enough spent in its alternating rounds of sleeping, eating, leisurely work and mild recreation. There is the sun too and the fresh salt air.

(R. H. Thornton: *British Shipping*, Cambridge University Press, 1959)

With the increasing introduction of automatic pilots, computerized navigation and automatic engine room controls, there will be a need for much less hard physical work—but even more skill.

General cargo ships have been replaced in importance by tankers—the biggest ships afloat. The oil tanker is the best known, but there are other tankers which carry cleaning fluids, chemicals, methane gas—even semi-liquid wood pulp, orange juice or wine! In 1970 tankers accounted for over five-ninths of Britain's total dead-weight tonnage. The first real oil tanker, a German ship, was launched in 1886. It was only 300 feet long, but the latest super-tanker, the *Globtik Tokyo*, launched in 1973, is over four times as long and is 238 252 gross tons. Tankers can carry 40 or 50 million tons of oil, and even larger ones are being planned. Life aboard an oil tanker in the 1950s was notorious for its boredom, although conditions have been considerably improved since then. (See Section 2.)

> 'Buffalo' Bill was young, but he had quite a history. First, he had spent a good deal too long in tankers. He had been to and from the Persian Gulf too many times; the silence, the monotony, the lack of drink or entertainment on board these ships is proverbial. Around them for weeks is the ocean; and their only reward at the end of the trip is a dirty bit of desert up the Gulf.
>
> (Robin King: *Sailor in the East,* Arthur Barker, 1956)

Since the 1950s completely new kinds of ships have been developed, including container ships in which cargo is carried in prepacked sealed metal boxes, to save handling costs in the docks. Container ships have no interior decks, but simply one vast hold in which the boxes are stored. But an even more radical development in the 1960s was the introduction of the straight-sided ship. The curves and rounded lines of traditional vessels have disappeared, apart from the bulging bows; instead the ship is made from prefabricated flat plates, thus greatly reducing the time needed to construct it. The first ship of this type was launched in Germany in 1968: in effect it is simply a gigantic floating warehouse, in which containers, or even cars, can be stacked one above another, side by side.

There have been equally revolutionary developments in the Royal Navy. The roll of warships, excluding smaller vessels, was very different in 1972–3 from what it was in 1945.

The Navy today is, of course, very much smaller than it was at the end of Britain's most total and exhausting war. But the composition of the fleet has changed radically, too. Battleships, which fought their only major contest at Jutland, have all disappeared. The sixty-two cruisers have been reduced to two, which are being converted into through-deck cruisers to carry helicopters. The fifty-two aircraft carriers have been reduced to one, though since then another one has been refitted. The frigate, of about 2 000 tons, has replaced the destroyer as the general factotum.

Type	Operational, preparing for service or engaged on trials and training	Reserve or undergoing long refit, conversion, etc.
Aircraft Carriers	1	
Commando Ships	2	1
Submarines	23	12
Assault Ships	2	
Cruisers	2	
Guided missile destroyers	6	3
Other destroyers	3	
General purpose frigates	25	8
Anti-aircraft frigates	3	1
Aircraft direction frigates	2	2
Anti-submarine frigates	23	1

(*Statement on the Defence Estimates*, H.M.S.O., 1972)

But the major change has been above and below the sea. Jet aircraft and helicopters like the Sea King, Wasp and Wessex now form an integral part of the Navy's strength. Developments below the sea have been even more important. Britain's first nuclear-powered submarine, the *Dreadnought,* was launched in 1960, in the same year as the United States' nuclear submarine *Triton* became the first to make an underwater voyage around the world. After the launching of Britain's first submarine equipped with Polaris missiles, the nuclear deterrent was in effect handed over from the Air Force to the Navy.

Barrow-in-Furness, September 15

Britain's first Polaris submarine, the Resolution, was launched today at Barrow, the dockyard which built the first submarine for the Navy....

The Resolution ... represents a fundamental change of life at sea undreamt of in traditional hearts of oak philosophy. Submariners will join the Navy not to see the world but to disappear from the world for two months at a time, visiting no foreign ports, sending out no messages, not showing the flag, down in the blind bottom of the ocean where there is no difference between night and day....

There the Resolution lay 7,000 tons and 400 feet of her, like an opulent black cigar.... 'The size of a light cruiser in the last war,' grunted the man from Vickers....

(*The Times*, 16th September 1966)

In the modern warship computers and electronics have replaced the old navigator's and gunner's skills. The naval rating of today, who handles equipment costing hundreds of thousands of pounds, is a highly educated technician.

The only kind of ship in which something of the old seafaring life still remains, in spite of all electronic aids, is the fishing-trawler, with its alternating three days in port and eleven days at sea.

The crew have had their time off in harbour—about three days—and the hour has arrived to start another trip. . . .

The passage to the fishing grounds is uncomfortable to say the least. Strong winds and heavy seas batter the trawler as it fights its way through the North Sea.

Apart from the normal watch duties the deck crew have to rig the trawl and get ready for fishing. This is done during a comparative lull in the weather, but even so the cold wind and freezing spray bite deep into the men working on the heaving deck. . . .

The trawling gear, which weighs about two tons, is shot and the crew know that there will now be little respite until the vessel stops fishing and heads for home. The monotonous procedure begins, shoot-haul, shoot-haul, shoot-haul every two or three hours day and night. Each haul produces up to two tons of cod and haddock which are gutted, washed and packed in ice in a fishroom. . . . The men work their usual long hours on deck and soon time has little meaning. . . . Eyes become sunken and red and the stubble of beards appears on haggard faces, for no one has time to shave.   Except for oilskins and boots, men tumble into their bunks fully clothed, for every minute of sleep is precious. . . .

The skipper, surrounded by modern navigational and fish-finding electronic aids, assesses and hunts.

(Bill Bridge: 'A Trawlerman describes a typical trip to the North Sea' in *Trident,* Official Newspaper of H.M. Dockyard, Portsmouth, August, 1969)

2

Since the end of the War conditions in both warships and merchant ships have improved out of all recognition. The minimum weekly scale of rations in merchant ships, in addition to such items as fish, vegetables and eggs, is:

Fresh water	7 gallons
Soft bread	7 lb

Flour	1 lb
Rice	6 oz
Oatmeal	6 oz
Fresh meat	$7\frac{1}{4}$ lb
Ham or bacon	12 oz
Potatoes	7 lb
Lentils, peas, beans, etc.	$1\frac{1}{2}$ lb
Onions	8 oz
Butter	$10\frac{1}{2}$ oz
Suet and cooking fats	6 oz
Sugar	$1\frac{1}{2}$ lb
Currants, sultanas, etc.	3 oz
Fruit	6 oz
Jams	8 oz
Cheese	5 oz
Tea	$4\frac{1}{2}$ oz
Coffee	2 oz

(Thornton, op. cit.)

There has also been a vast improvement in welfare and general amenities, pioneered in some cases by oil tankers in order to attract crews.

Children playing deck hockey on an educational cruise ship, *Uganda*.
P & O Shipping Line

The crew's swimming pool on a large oil tanker.

Shell

The tanker companies were among the first to introduce swimming pools, single berth cabins and film shows into their ships and, now that the rest of the Merchant Navy has followed suit, these companies will have to look for further improvements in order to attract men to their ships. This is all to the good for everyone at sea has benefited from the lead set by these companies.

(D. H. Moreby: *Personnel Management in Merchant Ships,* Pergamon Press, 1968)

An increasing number of merchant ships have recreation rooms, film shows, television, deck tennis and floodlit holds for sports. The Navy provides excellent amenities, too, with a great emphasis on sports of all kinds, and air-conditioned bunks, recreational rooms, and high-quality meals, with sometimes a choice of up to ten dishes for the main course, including steak or fresh salmon.

The ratings' galley on HMS *Juno*, 1973.

Ministry of Defence

H.M.S. Conqueror, the Royal Navy's fifth fleet nuclear submarine . . . is of 3 500 tons standard displacement, 285 feet in length. . . .

Her complement of 11 officers and 89 ratings will enjoy a high standard of accommodation with separate messes for senior and junior ratings on either side of a large modern galley, from which meals will be served on the cafeteria system.

Particular attention has been paid to the decor and furnishings of the living quarters and to the recreational facilities which will include cinema equipment and an extensive library of books and tape recordings to offset the monotony of prolonged underwater voyages.

Improved water distilling plant will provide unlimited fresh water for shower baths and the fully equipped laundry.

(*Trident,* October, 1969)

Discipline obviously has to be stricter in a ship than it does on land, as one man's neglect could endanger the lives of many others: a master of a merchant vessel still has the power to put a passenger ashore if he believes that his presence could cause trouble aboard. And crew members can be 'fined' a day's pay for such offences as drunkenness, disobedience of a lawful order, or using insolent or contemptuous language to an officer. And there is still an element of danger, too: fires, shipwrecks, and collisions still occur, in spite of all modern electronic aids.

But life at sea, with its own advantages and disadvantages, still has a great appeal to a particular kind of boy.

Approximately 80 per cent of ratings are recruited as boys between 16 and 17½ years of age. The majority of these receive 10 to 14 weeks' comprehensive pre-sea training, either as catering or deck boys, at the National Sea Training School, Gravesend, where the annual throughput is about 2 500. Some 200 are trained at other nautical establishments.
(*Opportunities in the Merchant Navy*, The British Shipping Federation, Ltd., n.d.)

Both the Merchant Navy and the Royal Navy are faced with the problem of retaining their recruits for a long period of service. Neither wants to keep a man, or a boy, who dislikes his work: in fact, it has never been easier to leave the Royal Navy than it is today. On the whole, the more highly qualified a man becomes, and the longer he stays on in the Service, the more likely he is to sign on for a further engagement. It is with men who have been at sea for several years only that the main problem arises.

One of the main factors in this wastage is what the Royal Navy calls the 'petticoat' influence. Once a man has married, his wife does not want him to be away from home for months or even weeks at a time. In the Merchant Navy more and more firms try to keep married couples in touch by flying out their letters by plane. A few companies are trying the experiment of allowing wives to accompany ratings on their voyages, as the wives of officers already do, but it provides a great problem in providing suitable accommodation. The Navy is considering the question of reducing the length of time that older men have to spend at sea, and is improving their accommodation.

Pay and conditions have never been better than they are today. A chief engineer on a relatively small cargo ship, for example, would have a minimum annual salary in excess of £3 276 and paid leave at the approximate rate of 136 days per year. In 1973 the basic national wage of an able seaman in a merchant vessel was £102 a month, plus 48 days' annual leave, but with overtime and special agreements many seamen earn much more—up to £50, or even £70 a week—and also get much longer annual leaves. In addition they have free food and accommodation aboard. Nevertheless, there have been two seamen's strikes in recent years, one in 1960 and another in 1966, lasting forty-seven days and finally involving 27 000 seamen and 900 ships.

3

Britannia no longer rules the waves. At the end of the last War the United States' Navy emerged as the largest and the most powerful in the world; the rapid expansion of the Russian Navy in the last decade has made it the second strongest. In 1972 there were nearly 80 000 officers and men, and 3 400 women, serving in the Royal Navy and the Royal Marines. Britain's merchant fleet now accounts for about one-tenth of the world's gross tonnage, but it includes the second largest fleet of tankers in the world. There are nearly 100 000 officers and men. Both navies remain essential—for the defence of the British Isles, and for importing and exporting the raw materials, food and manufactured goods on which the country depends.

As in other spheres, the pace of technological change has been extremely rapid in the post-War years, and it will go on at an accelerating pace. Ships will become even larger than they are now: one of the major advantages of the straight-plate, system-built ship is that it can be so easily lengthened. It only takes a week or so in dry dock for a new prefabricated section to be welded in between bow and stern. New materials may also be used more extensively in ship construction; already the Royal Navy has accepted into service a mine-hunter built of glass-reinforced plastic.

New methods of propulsion are also being used. In the 1920s oil started to replace coal; now over 80 per cent of the world's ships are oil-fuelled, which has virtually ended the dirty, exhausting job of fireman. Gas turbines and nuclear power are likely increasingly to replace oil. The American nuclear-powered merchant ship *Savannah* has been in operation since 1962, and nuclear power is also used for submarines. The Royal Navy is likely to run some of its surface ships on nuclear power as the United States Navy already does.

But the most important developments in the future may well occur below the surface of the sea and just above it. Already Britain's main defence is in the submarine world—with Polaris submarines and nuclear-powered submarine-hunters. The underwater area will become of increasing importance in many different ways: for navigation by echo-soundings on the mapped and charted ocean-bed; for exploitation of the untapped resources of the sea-bed; for discoveries by underwater archaeologists about the history of shipping; for experiments in underwater medicine; and even, perhaps—who knows?—for underwater 'hotels', where guests could observe all the strange forms of marine life.

John MacGregor keeping watch on the *Rob Roy*.
British Museum

Developments just above the surface of the waves may be of equal importance. The speed of ships has only doubled in the last hundred years. The hovercraft, invented by the British engineer Christopher—later Sir Christopher—Cockerell in 1953, opens the way to much higher speeds, by riding on an air cushion just above the surface of the sea, and thus avoiding the drag of water. Many technical problems still have to be overcome before large ocean-going, cargo hovercraft, capable of speeds of 100 knots or more, can be built, but some experts believe it possible.

But whatever happens in the future, the sea itself, and the small ships that now sail the oceans, will never lose their lure and fundamental appeal. Old forms of transport rarely die; they simply become the hobby, sport and passion of new generations. Even before steam had fully taken over from sail, one man had already set the pattern for solo voyages in small sailing-boats. John MacGregor didn't go very far in his 21-foot boat in 1867, only across the Channel, along the coast of France, up the river Seine, and back to England again. In the book that he wrote about his voyage, he enumerated some of the qualities that the lone sailor needed to possess.

> He must have good health and good spirits, and a passion for the sea. He must learn to ride, eat, drink, and sleep, as the water or winds decree, and not his watch. He must have wits to regard at once the tide, breeze, waves, chart, buoys, and lights; also the sails, Pilot-book, and compass; and more than all, to scan the passing vessels, and to cook, and eat, and drink in the midst of all. With such pressing and varied occupations, he has no time to feel 'lonely'.
> (John MacGregor: *The Voyage Alone in the Yawl 'Rob Roy'*, Hart-Davis, 1954)

MacGregor's voyage, his book, and his lectures had an instantaneous public appeal. The general fascination with such feats has continued, undiminished, from Joshua Slocum's single-handed voyage round the world in a 37-foot sloop in 1895–8, to the late Sir Francis Chichester's solo voyage in the 53-foot ketch *Gipsy Moth IV* in 1966–7. It seems unlikely that this fascination will ever fade: the mysteries, the adventure, the solace of the sea have a perennial appeal.

4

1886	First true oil tanker
c.1950	Container ships introduced
1960	*Dreadnought,* Britain's first nuclear-powered submarine
1960	US Navy submarine *Triton,* makes underwater voyage round the world
1960	Seamen's strike
1962	American nuclear-powered merchant ship, *Savannah,* enters service
1966	Seamen's strike
1966	*Resolution,* Britain's first Polaris submarine, launched
1966–7	Sir Francis Chichester's solo voyage in *Gipsy Moth*
1968	First system-built, straight-plate ship
1973	Oil tanker *Globtik Tokyo* 238 252 gross tons

General Bibliography

It is hoped that the extracts from numerous writers in the text will have given readers a chance to sample the flavour of the works cited, and encourage them to read on in some of them. Four recent books of particular interest dealing with the social history of the lower deck are:

Baynham, Henry, *From the Lower Deck: The Old Navy, 1780–1840*, Hutchinson, 1969

Kemp, Peter, *The British Sailor: A Social History of the Lower Deck*, Dent, 1971

Laffin, John, *Jack Tar: The Story of the British Sailor*, Cassell, 1969

Lloyd, Christopher, *The British Seaman, 1200–1860, A Social Survey*, Paladin, 1970

Other recent books of interest include:

Barnaby, K. C., *Some Ship Disasters and their Causes*, Hutchinson, 1968

Bass, George, *A History of Seafaring based on Under-water Archaeology*, Thames and Hudson, 1972

Bateson, Charles, *The Convict Ships, 1787–1868*, Brown, Son and Ferguson, 1959

Bathe, B. W., *British Warships, 1845–1945*, HMSO, 1970

Clowes, G. S. Laird, *Sailing Ships*, HMSO, 4th ed., 1952

Course, A. G., *The Merchant Navy: A Social History*, Muller, 1963

Davis, Ralph, *The Rise of the English Shipping Industry in the Seventeenth and Eighteenth Centuries*, Macmillan, 1962; David and Charles, 1972

Dickens, Admiral Sir Gerald, *The Dress of the British Sailor*, National Maritime Museum, HMSO, 1957

Featherstone, Donald Frederick, *Naval War Games: Fighting Sea Battles with Model Ships*, Stanley Paul, 1965

Guthrie, John, *Bizarre Ships of the Nineteenth Century*, Hutchinson, 1970

Hampshire, A. Cecil, *A Short History of the Royal Navy*, Director of Public Relations, Royal Navy, 1971

Hope, Ronald, *In Cabined Ships at Sea: Fifty Years of the Seafarers Education Service*, Harrap, 1969

Lewis, Michael Arthur, *The History of the British Navy*, Allen & Unwin, 1959

Miles, Stanley, *Underwater Medicine*, Staples Press, 2nd. ed., 1966

Piccard, Jacques and Dietz, R. S., *Seven Miles Down*, Longman, 1962

Pocock, R. F. and Garratt, G. R. M., *The Origins of Maritime Radio: The Story of the Introducion of wireless telegraphy in the Royal Navy between 1896 and 1900*, HMSO, 1972

Rogers, H. C. B., *Troopships and their History*, Seeley Service, 1963

Snow, Edward Rowe, *Sea Mysteries and Adventures*, Alvin Redman, 1964

——, *Women of the Sea*, Alvin Redman, 1963

Thornton, R. H., *British Shipping*, Cambridge University Press, 2nd. ed., 1959

Warner, Oliver, *Great Sea Battles*, Spring Books, 1969

EDUCATIONAL BOOKS

Claessen, J. M., *Voyages of Discovery*, Lutterworth, 1973

Ellacott, S. E., *Ships*, Methuen, 1958

Garrett, Richard, *Great Sea Mysteries*, Piccolo Books, 1971

Harland, S. J., *The Dustless Road: A Career in the Merchant Navy*, Educational Explorers, 1965

Hoare, R. J., *Travel by Sea*, A. & C. Black, 1967

McBride, Vonla, *Never at Sea: Life in the W.R.N.S.*, Educational Explorers, 1966

Palmer, Michael, *Ships and Shipping*, Batsford, 1971

Richardson, Patrick, *Nelson's Navy*, Longman, 1967

West, John, *A Captain in the Navy of Queen Anne*, Longman, 1970

For careers in the Merchant Navy contact the British Shipping Federation, Ltd, Shipping Federation House, 146–150 Minories, London EC3N 1ND. 'Acquaint visits' can be made to some establishments of the Royal Navy and the Royal Marines by careers masters, boys and girls, by contacting local careers officers—addresses under Naval Establishments in telephone directories.

SOCIETIES AND MUSEUMS

Birkenhead: Williamson Art Gallery and Museum, modern shipping and port of Merseyside.

Bristol: Brunel's *Great Britain*.

British Ship Adoption Society, (H.Q.) *Wellington,* Victoria Embankment, London, W.C.2., founded in 1936 to foster links between schools and also colleges and the ships and men of the Merchant Navy and, since 1969, the Royal Navy, by means of letters and visits. About 670 ships and schools are associated with the society.

Brixham: Brixham Museum, fishing, shipwright's tools, trawlers.

Dartmouth: Borough Museum, ship models.

Douglas, Isle of Man: Nautical Museum, fishing and trade in days of sail.

Great Yarmouth: Maritime Museum, East Anglian fishing, lifeboats.

Grimsby: Doughty Museum, ship models.

Hakluyt Society, c/o Birkbeck College, London, W.C.1., publishes records of voyages and naval expeditions.

London: H.M.S. *Discovery,* Scott's museum with relics of voyage. National Maritime Museum, Greenwich, with *Cutty Sark* and *Gipsy Moth IV* nearby.

H.M.S. *Belfast,* cruiser in the Pool of London.

Navy League, Broadway House, Broadway, London, S.W.19., educational and youth work for those with maritime interests. Publishes *Navy Magazine.*

Navy Records Society, c/o Royal Naval College, Greenwich, SE10 9NN, published very well-edited manuscripts and reprints of rare works—one of the major sources of maritime history.

Middlesbrough: Captain Cook Museum, photographs, models, etc.

Portsmouth: Nelson's *Victory.*

Redcar: Museum of Shipping and Fishing—also lifeboats.

Seafarers Education Service and College of the Sea, Mansbridge House, 207 Balham High Road, London SW17 7BH, voluntary society founded in 1919 to provide a library service and general education for merchant seamen. Welcomes gifts of good books and magazines, and uses mainly qualified teachers as voluntary tutors for seamen. Publishes the *Seafarer.*

Society for Nautical Research, National Maritime Museum, Greenwich, SE10 9FF, publishes *Mariner's Mirror,* the eminent journal of naval history.

Southampton: Wool House Maritime Museum, local and general shipping history.

World Ship Society, 10 Romney Avenue, Kendal, Westmorland, for those interested in ships of all ages and types. Publishes *Marine News.*

Glossary

The more unusual terms are explained in footnotes, but the meanings of some more common maritime words and terms are explained below. (For a comprehensive glossary see René de Ker-chove, *International Maritime Dictionary*, Macmillan, 1948. Wilfred Granville, *A Dictionary of Sailor's Slang*, Deutsch, 1962, is also very useful.)

Able seaman, originally a man who was able to 'hand, reef and steer'; now an efficient, skilled and experienced deck-hand.

Aft, at or near the *stern.*

Ballast, weight put in a ship's hold to balance the weight of the superstructure, when it has no cargo, or too little to make it stable. Stone, sand, gravel was often used in the past; now it is usually metal, or water or oil in tanks.

Barque, a three to five-masted sailing vessel, *square rigged* on the forward masts only.

Bilges, the space in the lower part of the ship's hold, where waste water collects.

Boatswain, pronounced bo'sun, and commonly spelt in that way, a petty officer in charge of deck-hands, who has a special whistle emitting different sounds to indicate specific tasks. In modern vessels, men are 'piped' to work by internal broadcast systems.

Bow, the front part of a vessel.

Brig, a two-masted, *square-rigged* sailing-ship.

Brigantine, a two-masted sailing vessel, *square rigged* on forward mast and *fore and aft rigged* on mainmast.

Bulwark, the woodwork or plating along the sides of a vessel, which helps to keep the decks dry and to stop objects—and men—from falling overboard.

Capstan, a mechanical device used for raising the anchor and lifting heavy weights.

Deadweight tonnage is the amount, expressed in tons, that a ship can carry in cargo, fuel, passengers etc.

Displacement tonnage usually means the weight of a ship at its normal full load.

Draught, see *Load lines.*

Fore and aft rigged, when the sails extend roughly parallel to the *keel* to the *lee* side of the vessel.

Forecastle, pronounced fo'c's'le, and usually written in that way, originally a raised platform at *bow,* from which the soldiers on board fought enemy vessels, now a short superstructure over the forward part of a vessel, where the crew sometimes lives.

Galley, historically a small, low boat usually rowed by slaves, criminals or captured sailors; a ship's kitchen or cook house.

Gross tonnage is a measure of the internal cargo-carrying capacity of a ship, one ton being equivalent to 100 cubic feet.

Gunwale, the upper edge of a vessel's side.

Hatchway, an opening in a deck giving access to the space, hold or deck below.

Jack Tar, a common name for a sailor, probably originating in the abbreviation of 'jacket' to 'jack' and the use of tar to make the jackets waterproof.

Keel, the lowest plates or timber, running fore and aft along the whole length of a vessel; the 'backbone' of a vessel.

Ketch, a small two-masted sailing vessel, often used in coastal navigation.

Lee, the sheltered side of a vessel, opposite to the *weather side.*

Load lines, indicate the level to which a ship can be safely loaded. The first, and the best known, is the Plimsoll mark—a circle bisected by a line—but there are now often other load lines showing load limits for various sea conditions and areas. The series of numbers at the *bow* and *stern* show the draught, the distance in feet or metres between the waterline and the *keel.*

Masts are composed of several sections in larger vessels. Above the lower mast comes the top mast, then the topgallant, and the royal. The foremast is the first mast, near the bow; the mainmast is the tallest; and the mizzen mast, in a three-masted vessel, comes between the mainmast and the *stern.*

Mess, a group of men who eat together; the place where they do so.

Ordinary seaman, a man who has not qualified as an *able seaman.*

Plimsoll mark, see *Load lines.*

Poop, a raised deck by the *stern,* connected by a stairway in naval vessels to the *quarterdeck.*

Port, the left-hand side of a vessel looking forward.

Purser, historically the officer in a naval vessel responsible for supplies of provisions and clothing; now an officer in a merchant ship responsible for ship's books, etc.

Quarterdeck, the upper deck from the mainmast to the break of the *poop* or the *stern,* reserved for officers.

Rigging, all the ropes, chains, etc. used for supporting sails.

Shrouds, ropes or wires extending from the masthead to the sides of the ship, to support the masts.

Sloop, small one-masted, *fore and aft rigged* vessel.

Slop clothing, ready-made clothing.

Square rigged, having the main sails square and set at right angles to the *keel,* as opposed to *fore and aft rigging.*

Starboard, the right-hand side of a vessel looking forward.

Stern, the afterpart of a vessel.

Top, a platform at the top of the lower *mast,* used for observation, and formerly for soldiers to fire down on an enemy's decks.

Topgallant forecastle, a short deck forward above the upper deck, which provided roomier accommodation for crews.

Victuals, provisions, food.

Watch, the period of duty, four hours on and four hours off; the men who are working on that shift.

Weather side, from which the wind is blowing.

Yard, a spar, or pole, slung across the mast to support the sail.

Index